ANNE BRONTË:
A New Critical Assessment

ANNE BRONTË:
A New Critical Assessment

by
P. J. M. Scott

VISION
and
BARNES & NOBLE

Vision Press Limited
Fulham Wharf
Townmead Road
London SW6 2SB

and

Barnes & Noble Books
81 Adams Drive
Totowa, NJ 07512

ISBN (UK) 0 85478 275 3
ISBN (US) 0 389 20345 9

Printed and bound in Great Britain by
Unwin Brothers Ltd.,
Old Woking, Surrey.
Phototypeset by Galleon Photosetting,
Ipswich, Suffolk.
MCMLXXXIII

Contents

Introduction

In the only sense which ultimately matters Anne Brontë has not been read. That explains her eclipse, the small minority of supporters and admirers she enjoys (as to real keenness of discipleship) and the phrases of ritual attention and dismissal which still form themselves, almost from force of habit now, in the literary histories.

The reasons for these things are readily penetrable. She offers a different vision of life from her sisters' works *and* a vision not all that congenial to the 135 years since she published. 1847–1982 has not been the best of epochs in which to be a specifically Christian writer—working out, however freshly and honestly, religious themes in a social aspect. It is a hindrance to repute the more if side by side with this activity—though she is as good a novelist as some Christians were poets during the Renaissance—your achievement sits in such close proximity beside other *oeuvres*, Charlotte's and Emily's, different indeed in tone and direction (though there are many things of course the Brontë sisters agree about—e.g. anger against Calvinism, all forms of tyranny) and answering much more fully to the intervening age's view of itself: a view, needless to say, not in all points discerning and accurate.

My own feeling is that it takes all types etc. and, though in the very last analysis I have certain small reservations, expressed towards the end of these pages, about the ultimate 'tendencies' of her sisters' *opera*, I offer myself as committed in active, nourishment-gaining admiration of *Wuthering Heights* and *Jane Eyre*, *Villette*, Emily's poems and the other Brontë works as any fanatic could desire. But the case for seeing in those texts some of the most illuminating virile writing and human expostulation in our literature has already been well canvassed by able hands and most percipient attentions.

What seems ironically unjust to the point of conspiracy is

6

the scant treatment (in the main) poor Anne has enjoyed in critical appreciation—'poor' only in the after-history given to her work, for she is herself as great a writer as her sisters; just significantly different.

Agnes Grey makes a substantial statement about life and is perfect. The poems constitute an impressive opus, all the more so if read sequentially as one work, the spiritual autobiography of an individual coming to terms with love, frustration and death. The letters, few as they are, are astonishing—documents almost in a case-history of sanctity (I mean the genuine article, that 'condition about which Theology has nothing to say', no cloying pious self-consciousness of any wrong kind whatever). They alone, taken with the biographical facts, should provoke a pondering respect of no small duration. And *The Tenant of Wildfell Hall*: well, though this has its weak elements, it is the shocking power and comprehensiveness of its *procédé* that ought to fill most of our vista.

In a specialized sense which I think one can define Anne was a 'born novelist' as her siblings were not. With *Wuthering Heights* Emily offers a unique, totally unrepeatable or extendable sport. Charlotte is a sort of literary Mahler, working and reworking one kind of experience and protest (in her case, to put the matter crudely, 'feminist'). When, in *Shirley*, she sets her hand to other materials than the passionally tormented intelligent woman and her inadequate role in society, she shows forth at her weakest. The crudity of those accounts, the audacity of such drastic shrifts, I acknowledge in letting them stand simply for the sake of making a point which refers not at all to the stature of these various achievements: that Anne was a novelist (the evidence certifies this from all parts of her compass) as was Henry James; or as Shakespeare was a poet-dramatist—an artist of extraordinary powers who, while opportunity offered, developed, changed, amplified her subject-matter and her means of expression. If there were anything but impious fatuity in the utterance, one would say that she alone of English literary history's *makars* would have had more work of the most substantial kind to show, inevitably, than what she was allotted time for. On that issue even Jane Austen and Keats abide our question: she is free. Each new work (and she adverts to her intention of future products only a month before her death) would have been a development, a new horizon transmitted, a piling of harvest after harvest in great artistic act upon act. On that we can all stake every bottom dollar.

But my text does not address itself to jibbing at the Providence which gives us all far better than we deserve or want—which gives us what we need (though that truth is too severe to bear contemplation much of the time and is most patronizing and repugnant thus penned by mere mortal hand). I am concerned with the actual legacy which long since ought to have enjoyed a high place in the Pantheon of literary esteems: and for its nutrient, corrective vitalities of feeling and insight.

One wants to cry out like Mrs. Warren Hope in 'The Abasement of the Northmores'. What on earth have we all been playing at so to neglect *this* moral repast, this intellectual illumination? We must have been mad, with the principal lunacy which prevails in human affairs; deafness to just the voices, the words that their given era needs most to hear.

Since there are no sufficiently scholarly-established texts of Anne Brontë's novels, I quote from them simply by chapter and trust to the reader's finding the passages in question transcribed more or less in the same state in his own edition. We now all have the benefit, however, of Mr. Edward Chitham's *The Poems of Anne Brontë: A New Text and Commentary* (London, 1979), which ought to be the standard volume for a long time to come, and reference to the poems is made from that book. The letters, variously reprinted, I quote out of the texts perhaps most readily available—in Miss Gérin's biography (revised edition of 1976).

1

Agnes Grey:
Accommodating Reality

Agnes Grey has three principal purposes: a paedogogic one; a
protest against tyranny; and an attempt to reconcile the
passionate yearning heart with life's realities, with its actual
possibilities.

We underrate the novel if its brevity and simplicity of
construction cause us to think the handling of these themes is
slight.

As a story it is simple enough. The eponymous young
heroine, who narrates the whole, grows up in a good-natured
loving North of England family, the daughter of a clergyman,
who loses on a business speculation even the 'snug little
property of his own' which has amplified hitherto their modest
circumstances. As well as making drastic retrenchments the
family now considers ways and means of supplementing his
meagre stipend. Mrs. Grey suggests to the older of her two
surviving children Mary the drawing of pictures for sale.
Agnes herself volunteers to become a governess and after
much opposition from the other members of the household
carries her point.

> At last, to my great joy, it was decreed that I should take charge
> of the young family of a certain Mrs. Bloomfield; whom my
> kind, prim aunt Grey had known in her youth, and asserted to
> be a very nice woman. Her husband was a retired tradesman,
> who had realised a very comfortable fortune; but could not be
> prevailed upon to give a greater salary than twenty-five pounds
> to the instructress of his children. I, however, was glad to

9

accept this, rather than refuse the situation—which my parents were inclined to think the better plan.

After a long cold journey in the middle of the succeeding September, she arrives at the Bloomfields' mansion Wellwood only to discover chilly hospitality from the mistress of the house and that its children are undisciplined cruel egotists. Tom (aged 7), Mary Ann (almost 6) and Fanny (almost 4 on their new preceptress's coming) are her charges and heavy work they make for her. The parents expect Agnes Grey to keep these artful savages in order, having themselves indulged them all along and continuing to impose no settled course of restraints and encouragements of their own.

Tom indeed has the most barbarous instincts towards animals, and retails 'a list of torments' he intends to inflict upon 'a brood of little callow nestlings' which he has just filched from a neighbouring plantation, but

> while he was busied in the relation, I dropped the stone upon his intended victims and crushed them flat beneath it. Loud were the outcries, terrible the execrations, consequent upon this daring outrage. . . .
>
> But soon my trials in this quarter came to a close—sooner than I either expected or desired; for one sweet evening towards the close of May, as I was rejoicing in the near approach of the holidays, and congratulating myself upon having made some progress with my pupils (as far as their learning went at least, for I *had* instilled *something* into their heads, and I had at length brought them to be a little—a very little—more rational about getting their lessons done in time to leave some space for recreation, instead of tormenting themselves and me all day long to no purpose), Mrs. Bloomfield sent for me, and calmly told me that after Midsummer my services would be no longer required. She assured me that my character and general conduct were unexceptionable; but the children had made so little improvement since my arrival, that Mr. Bloomfield and she felt it their duty to seek some other mode of instruction. Though superior to most children of their years in abilities, they were decidedly behind them in attainments: their manners were uncultivated, and their tempers unruly. And this she attributed to a want of sufficient firmness, and diligent, persevering care on my part. (Ch. 5)

This failure Agnes actually finds disappointing, but with fresh hope she sets out on another governess-employment, gained by placing an advertisement of her qualifications in the newspapers. It takes her (at £50 a year) to

> the family of Mr. Murray, of Horton Lodge, near O——, about seventy miles from our village: a formidable distance to me, as I had never been above twenty miles from home in all the course of my twenty years' sojourn on earth; and as, moreover, every individual in that family and in the neighbourhood was utterly unknown to myself and all my acquaintances. But this rendered it only the more piquant to me.

It turns out, however, that Horton Lodge is far from being a sanctuary of sweetness and light. Here again her employers have a very limited sense of her identity and needs as a human being. Mr. Murray is largely absent from her purview, a blusterous red-faced portly country gent. His wife is a giddy social butterfly, chiefly concerned, in the later phases of the story, about making 'good' matches for her two daughters—at whatever such trifling cost as matrimonial misery.

These girls and their brothers also, like the Bloomfields, have been 'outrageously spoiled', so that 'Master Charles . . . his mother's peculiar darling . . . was . . . only active in doing mischief, and only clever in inventing falsehoods: not simply to hide his faults, but, in mere malicious wantonness, to bring odium upon others.' However, of both boys' instruction and management the new governess is delivered twelve months after her arrival by the dispatch of the younger to follow his brother at a boarding school.

At all times and seasons the youngsters torment Miss Grey with their selfish irrational conduct, and by all the family her convenience or comfort is never consulted. Likewise the local squirearchy never speaks to her or takes any notice of her existence and in Mr. Hatfield, the vicar of the parish, Anne Brontë satirizes much that she despised and hated in the Established Church of her days—among other things, the alternation between sermons 'sunless and severe' and ingratiation of wealthy parishioners. Yet Agnes is comforted to note how the new curate, Mr. Edward Weston, nowise resembles him.

11

Meanwhile she receives a blow-by-blow account from day to day of the intrigues in cynical flirtation, and for heartless marriage, on the part of her elder charge Rosalie Murray, who aims at rich wedlock to a baronet while teasing both the parson and Harry Meltham, a younger son of the local hall.

Visiting one Nancy Brown, an elderly pauper of the village, who, as well as by physical disablement has been 'somewhat afflicted with religious melancholy' (Ch. 11), Agnes has learned of Mr. Weston's good offices as a comforting pastor in this household of hidden suffering. And indeed she finds that the new young curate, not specially winsome in his ways or of his person as he is, has done like offices in other poor homes, including material help:

> 'Just for all the world!' exclaimed his [a poor consumptive labourer's] wife; 'an about a three wik sin', when he seed how poor Jem shivered wi' cold, an' what pitiful fires we kept, he axed if wer stock of coals was nearly done. I told him it was, an' we was ill set to get more: but you know, mum, I didn't think o' him helping us; but howsever, he sent us a sack o' coals next day; an' we've had good fires ever sin: an' a great blessing it is, this winter time. But that's his way, Miss Grey: when he comes into a poor body's house a seein' sick folk, he like notices what they most stand i'need on; an' if he thinks they can't readily get it therseln, he never says nowt about it, but just gets it for 'em. An' it isn't everybody 'at 'ud do that, 'at has as little as he has: for you know, mum, he's now't at all to live on but what he gets fra' th' rector, an' that's little enough, they say.'

It comes as all the harder to bear for the plain governess (as she deems herself) when Rosalie Murray with her very real beauty and charm exercises the idle prenuptial time of her espousal to Sir Thomas Ashby in attempting to engage the curate's affections as well; since by then Agnes has thoroughly fallen in love with Mr. Weston and highly esteems his quiet virtue, strength of character, courage and independence of spirit.

This last quality appears uppermost, for all that Weston has occasionally taken the opportunity of walking with, talking to Miss Grey and plucking flowers for her, when he bears very calmly the news of her departure from Horton following the death of her father back at home and the resolution there taken by mother and daughter to hire and conduct a ladies' seminary in a coastal resort at the other side of the county. (Her sister Mary is by now married to a poor parson of her own.)

As the weeks pass with no further word coming from him, Agnes abandons the faint hope raised by his last question (' "It is possible we may meet again," said he; "will it be of any consequence to you whether we do or not?" '); and she accepts the erewhile Rosalie Murray's invitation to stay at Ashby Park. There she observes the beginning of a life of married unhappiness which exhibits a new pathos in the bride's fate, even as or though that young woman herself is bored with her infant child.

Back at the watering-place which is now scene of both home and work to her, Agnes goes one summer morning early for 'a solitary ramble on the sands while half the world was in bed'. Here she encounters Weston again and it turns out he 'never could discover' her address, that he has lately been installed in a living only two miles distant. He visits her and her mother from now on regularly, and one evening taking her for a walk towards a cliff with a magnificent sea-view, he proposes.

With their marriage and a restrospective summary of their happiness over subsequent years, as co-workers in the church and as parents of three children no less than as partners, the tale concludes.

Stated like that the story is bald and bare to the point of banality; and indeed the anticlimactic mood or effect of its closing phase is something which deserves attention. But two things give the whole a solidity and value quite out of the run-of-the-mill. First, the substantiality of its heroine's nature, which is mediated to us by the quality of her language as narrator. And second, deriving from this, the amount of ground the book covers in its brief compass.

Ars est celare artem. A wholly perspicuous literary style is one of the highest attainments, whether conscious or 'given', of a writer. To create a complete picture of a living world 'out there' in front of your readers by linguistic means of which they are unaware or rendered unobservant—well, the power to do that inheres only in a few classics, let alone lesser works.

Some great authors are justly valued for the idiosyncrasy of their style: a chief value in reading them is contact with the highly individual voice which their pages offer—say those of Sir Thomas Browne or Jeremy Taylor, Marcel Proust or the later Henry James. But the other, the 'quiet thing', is much more difficult of achievement.

Anne Brontë's narrative manner operates like a transparent pane of glass. We stare straight through it at the subjects under consideration.

> All true histories contain instruction; though, in some, the treasure may be hard to find, and when found, so trivial in quantity, that the dry, shrivelled kernel scarcely compensates for the trouble of cracking the nut. Whether this be the case with my history or not, I am hardly competent to judge. I sometimes think that it might prove useful to some, and entertaining to others; but the world may judge for itself. Shielded by my own obscurity, and by the lapse of years, and a few fictitious names, I do not fear to venture; and will candidly lay before the public what I would not disclose to the most intimate friend.

Thus the very opening of the novel.

This is not hemming and hawing, a proemial warming-up which, for all the good it does, could just as well be cut. We need to be supplied with a motive for what follows—for why is Agnes Grey telling her story? Yet we don't want a prologomenon which testifies to nothing so much as its author's self-importance with either blatant arrogance or coy pseudo-apology; and neither type of effusion is here traceable.

The narrative is confessedly offered as having a didactic drift and potential moralistic value, but in a direct quiet manner which is self-conscious in all the right ways and none of the wrong ones. To this the absence of any turgid lumbering in the style testifies; indeed negatives will characterize the best terms of our praise for this side of Anne Brontë's accomplishment, and just because it is so thoroughly accomplished. Those first four sentences are paced so as to move with a light various rhythm; but not to draw attention to themselves as so doing. Though their declared focus is the historian herself we have already become unconscious, by the end of that short paragraph, of a mind behind it manipulating a rhetoric.

14

As we drove along, my spirits revived again, and I turned, with
pleasure, to the contemplation of the new life upon which I was
entering. But though it was not far past the middle of September, the heavy clouds and strong north-easterly wind combined
to render the day extremely cold and dreary; and the journey
seemed a very long one, for, as Smith observed, the roads were
'very heavy'; and certainly, his horse was very heavy too: it
crawled up the hills, and crept down them, and only condescended to shake its sides in a trot where the road was at a
dead level or a very gentle slope, which was rarely the case in
those rugged regions; so that it was nearly one o'clock before we
reached the place of our destination. Yet, after all, when we
entered the lofty iron gateway, when we drove softly up the
smooth, well-rolled carriage road, with the green lawn on each
side, studded with young trees, and approached the new but
stately mansion of Wellwood, rising above its mushroom
poplar-groves, my heart failed me, and I wished it were a mile
or two farther off. For the first time in my life, I must stand
alone: there was no retreating now. I must enter that house,
and introduce myself among its strange inhabitants. But how
was it to be done? True, I was near nineteen; but, thanks to my
retired life and the protecting care of my mother and sister, I
well knew that many a girl of fifteen, or under, was gifted with a
more womanly address, and greater ease and self-possession,
than I was. Yet, if Mrs. Bloomfield were a kind, motherly
woman, I might do very well, after all; and the children, of
course, I should soon be at ease with them—and Mr. Bloomfield, I hoped, I should have but little to do with. (The opening
of Ch. 2)

The balance here of narrative, description, commentary and
self-revelation is very finely judged. We move without effort
from the young appointee's inward musings to the exterior
scene, first in its totality and then particulars—as her new
place of work swings into view; then back again to the interior
ponderings which have now (at the crisis of the journey as it
were) become self-examination. Look how different the devices
are which make actual to us the horse's gait, the pace of the
journey, on the one hand, and on the other the effect of the
whole new Wellwood topography upon its present recruit's
eye and spirit. 'Condescended to shake its sides in a trot' is a
lovely mimesis, full of close observation and gentle irony where

the paratactic sentence with a very simple structure of clauses also conveys the laboured progress the travellers enjoy. Which is immediately followed by the rather breathless rhythm of the prose at the entrance to the grounds of Agnes's new abode:

(1) Yet, (after all) . . .
(2) when we entered . . .
   (2a) when we drove . . .
   (2a/i) with the green lawn . . .
   (2a/iA) studded with young trees,
(3) and approached
   (3a) rising above . . .

The dependency of these numerous clauses one upon another, the accumulation of them before the wave of the sentence breaks at 'my heart failed me' (its main verb), well conveys the rising apprehension, even to panic, of the new arrival.

We move at once into quick *erlebte Rede*:

> For the first time in my life, I must stand alone: there was no retreating now. I must enter that house, and introduce myself among its strange inhabitants. But how was it to be done?

At the remove of only one tense this is her self-address of the actual historical moment; provoking in its turn a reflection on her general situation, her identity as a social being altogether, in the more relaxed amplitude of which we are given two points of view: the young woman's, little more than a girl, to whom all this happened at the original time, and that of the more experienced judicious narrator of after years who is telling her tale. ('True, I was near nineteen, etc. . . .')

This very fluency of representational competence all but matches Dickens's art on like occasions in his first-person-told *Bildungsromane, David Copperfield* and *Great Expectations*; so that there seeps into our subconscious the conviction that a narrator, who has speech and therefore life itself so much under her hand and is such a true reflector of the world, possesses in herself a human value which makes important the novel's trajectory of its old theme, innocence passing through experience.

The duality of vision—the older Agnes mediates to us the

experiences of her younger self—is in the main handled with secure success. There are, at least for me, only a couple of instances where uncertainty obtrudes. Is there a cringing kittenishness in the heroine's speech and attitude during the second half of Chapter 1? Is it that, recording the same, the novelist is using the quietly ironic eye she deploys upon other human weakness in her pages? Or is it simply truthful psychological portraiture; is this exactly how her heroine would speak and move, in consequence of a life spent hitherto in greatly sheltered innocence? We may be the more wary of censuring this first of such 'lapses', if that is what they be, given the truly virile range and variety of tone—the moral insight and control—in the paragraphs preceding it.

Likewise with a certain moment in Chapter 11:

> One bright day in the last week of February, I was walking in the park, enjoying the threefold luxury of solitude, a book, and pleasant weather; for Miss Matilda had set out on her daily ride, and Miss Murray was gone in the carriage with her mamma to pay some morning calls. But it struck me that I ought to leave these selfish pleasures, and the park with its glorious canopy of bright blue sky, the west wind sounding through its yet leafless branches, the snow-wreaths still lingering in its hollows, but melting fast beneath the sun, and the graceful deer browsing on its moist herbage already assuming the freshness and verdure of spring—and go to the cottage of one Nancy Brown, a widow, whose son was at work all day in the fields, and who was afflicted with an inflammation in the eyes. . . .

The governess here strikes me as being somewhat—and the least bit disagreeably—'pi'. Such pleasures as appreciating Nature's glories are not 'selfish' but of themselves wholesome; at least, in a life not given up to indulgence and sloth, which anyway has few enjoyments or releases in it. There is arguably a kind of embarrassment on the narrator's part herself communicated to us in the way the sentence that conveys the new resolution to visit the cottager is worked up with a lengthy subordination of clauses, to end so (as it were) consciously in bathos (indicated no less with the hyphenation which introduces the closing cadences). Perhaps this is again simple psychological fidelity on Anne Brontë's part: at a time when her personality is under assault from various angles, Agnes Grey is attempting to shore it up and find refuge in deliberate self-conscious rectitude. Her problem at Horton Lodge is that everything there constitutes a continual raid on her self-esteem. We may be offered here, archly from the narrator's view, a glimpse of her method for compensation. But we are not sure. The tale as a whole is not told in a mode, like Jane Austen's, which alerts us *all the time* to the smallest nuances of tone as likely to be critical of the heroine's motivations, in however fugitive, slight and complex a fashion.

Complex but assured in its disposition of tones is the episode of the primroses, the symbolic moment in which Edward Weston indicates his concern for Miss Grey and even a particular interest in her.

> Whether I walked with the young ladies or rode with their parents [to church of a Sunday], depended upon their own capricious will: if they chose to 'take' me, I went; if, for reasons best known to themselves, they chose to go alone, I took my seat in the carriage. I liked walking better, but a sense of reluctance to obtrude my presence on any one who did not desire it, always kept me passive on these and similar occasions; and I never inquired into the causes of their varying whims. Indeed, this was the best policy—for to submit and oblige was the governess's part, to consult their own pleasure was that of the pupils. But when I did walk, the first half of the journey was generally a great nuisance to me. As none of the before-mentioned ladies and gentlemen ever noticed me, it was disagreeable to walk beside them, as if listening to what they said, or wishing to be thought one of them, while they talked over me, or across; and if their eyes, in speaking, chanced to fall on me, it seemed as if they looked on vacancy—as if they either did not see me, or were very desirous to make it appear so. It was disagreeable, too, to walk behind, and thus appear to acknowledge my own inferiority; for, in truth, I considered myself pretty nearly as good as the best of them, and wished them to know that I did so, and not to imagine that I looked upon myself as a mere domestic, who knew her own place too well to walk beside such fine ladies and gentlemen as they were—though her young ladies might choose to have her with them, and even condescend to converse with her when no better company were at hand. Thus—I am almost ashamed to confess it—but indeed I gave myself no little trouble in my

18

endeavours (if I did keep up with them) to appear perfectly unconscious or regardless of their presence, as if I were wholly absorbed in my own reflections, or the contemplation of surrounding objects; or, if I lingered behind, it was some bird or insect, some tree or flower, that attracted my attention, and having duly examined that, I would pursue my walk alone, at a leisurely pace, until my pupils had bidden adieu to their companions, and turned off into the quiet, private road.

One such occasion I particularly well remember: it was a lovely afternoon about the close of March; Mr. Green and his sisters had sent their carriage back empty, in order to enjoy the bright sunshine and balmy air in a sociable walk home along with their visitors, Captain Somebody and Lieutenant Somebody else (a couple of military fops), and the Misses Murray, who, of course, contrived to join them. Such a party was highly agreeable to Rosalie; but not finding it equally suitable to my taste, I presently fell back, and began to botanise and entomologise along the green banks and budding hedges, till the company was considerably in advance of me, and I could hear the sweet song of the happy lark; then my spirit of misanthropy began to melt away beneath the soft, pure air and genial sunshine: but sad thoughts of early childhood, and yearnings for departed joys, or for a brighter future lot, arose instead. As my eyes wandered over the steep banks covered with young grass and green-leaved plants, and surmounted by budding hedges, I longed intensely for some familiar flower that might recall the woody dales or green hillsides of home: the brown moorlands, of course, were out of the question. Such a discovery would make my eyes gush out with water, no doubt; but that was one of my greatest enjoyments now. At length I descried, high up between the twisted roots of an oak, three lovely primroses, peeping so sweetly from their hiding-place that the tears already started at the sight; but they grew so high above me that I tried in vain to gather one or two, to dream over and to carry with me: I could not reach them unless I climbed the bank, which I was deterred from doing by hearing a footstep at that moment behind me, and was, therefore, about to turn away, when I was startled by the words, 'Allow me to gather them for you, Miss Grey,' spoken in the grave low tones of a well-known voice. Immediately the flowers were gathered, and in my hand. It was Mr. Weston, of course— who else would trouble himself to do so much for *me*? (Ch. 13)

We are shown several of the concomitants when a human being is treated as a convenience, not as a full independent entity with a valued life. As her companions look through or talk over her, Agnes has no socially recognized means of reacting which repudiates her loss of status and yet which does not itself denigrate her. Even *feeling* resentment is demeaning, because it acknowledges a hurt and that means living at the standards and level of this third-rate company itself. Yet not to feel it, nor to attempt showing it in any way, would seem a loss of caste as a human identity; perhaps cowardly also, possibly too quietist in attitude.

It is a poisoning air Agnes Grey breathes at Horton, bringing decay into all aspects of her own nature, which cannot wholly be separated off (this is Anne Brontë's point) as something intrinsically distinct from her environment and *its* morality. It may well put us in mind of Fanny Price's dilemma at Mansfield Park, the predicament that is her entire role there—or of any good Austen character faced with delinquency in a constricted unalterable and inescapable social group. She is imprisoned and the impossibility of dealing wholly healthfully with the pressures upon her is illustrated for us in several features of this 'sequence'.

First of all there is the backbiting cattiness that mars her account of her young charges' visiting swains: 'Captain Somebody and Lieutenant Somebody else (a couple of military fops)'. This governess has a score of big just grievances against the Misses Murray, but we see resentment turning to general misanthropy in parlance so dismissive of those identities. And she who was once like a saint from Olympus in comparison with the mentality of her pupils begins, oppressed by their injustice, to sound like a cantankerous gossip of no elevated mind at all: 'for, in truth, I considered myself pretty nearly as good as the best of them, and wished them to know that I did so, and not to imagine that I looked upon myself as a mere domestic, who knew her own place too well to walk beside such fine ladies and gentlemen as they were—'.

That is not so very far off the internal chatter of Mrs. Petito, the lady's maid in Maria Edgeworth's *The Absentee* (published 1812, a novel which almost certainly Anne Brontë had read in her formative years):

'It will do very well, never mind,' repeated Petito, muttering to herself as she looked after the ladies whilst they ran downstairs,

'I can't abide to dress any young lady who says never mind, and it will do very well. That, and her never talking to one confidentially, or trusting one with the least bit of her secrets, is the thing I can't put up with from Miss Nigent; and Miss Broadhurst holding the pins to me, as much as to say, do your business, Petito, and don't talk. Now, that's so impertinent, as if one wasn't the same flesh and blood, and had not as good a right to talk of everything, and hear of everything, as themselves. And Mrs. Broadhurst, too, cabinet councilling with my lady, and pursing up her city mouth, when I come in, and turning off the discourse to snuff, forsooth, as if I was an ignoramus, to think they closeted themselves to talk of snuff. Now, I think a lady of quality's woman has as good a right to be trusted with her lady's secrets as with her jewels; and if my Lady Clonbrony was a real lady of quality, she'd know that, and consider the one as much my paraphernalia as the other. So I shall tell my lady tonight, as I always do when she vexes me, that I never lived in an Irish family before, and don't know the ways of it. Then she'll tell me she was born in Hoxfordshire; then I shall say, with my saucy look, "Oh, was you, my lady? I always forget that you was an Englishwoman." Then maybe she'll say "Forget! you forget yourself strangely, Petito." Then I shall say, with a great deal of dignity, "If your ladyship thinks so, my lady, I'd better go." And I'd desire no better than that she would take me at my word, for my Lady Dashfort's is a much better place, I'm told, and she's dying to have me, I know.'

Mrs. Petito is much more amusing and less justified in her situation than Agnes Grey in hers, yet a similar note is discernible in the musings of the latter heroine upon her wrongs, a kind of bleat-bleat-bleat of, itself, no very elevated mind.

In *Reflections on the Psalms* C. S. Lewis referred to what is centrally in question here:

It seemed to me that, seeing in them [the cursings in the Psalms] hatred undisguised, I saw also the natural result of injuring a human being. The word *natural* is here important. This result can be obliterated by grace, suppressed by prudence or social convention, and (which is dangerous) wholly disguised by self-deception. But just as the natural result of throwing a lighted match into a pile of shavings is to produce a fire—though damp or the intervention of some more sensible person may prevent it—so the natural result of cheating a man, or 'keeping him down' or neglecting him, is to arouse resentment;

21

that is, to impose upon him the temptation of becoming what the Psalmists were when they wrote the vindictive passages. He may succeed in resisting the temptation; or he may not. If he fails, if he dies spiritually because of his hatred for me, how do I, who provoked that hatred, stand? For in addition to the original injury I have done him a far worse one. I have introduced into his inner life, at best a new temptation, at worst a new besetting sin. If that sin utterly corrupts him, I have in a sense debauched or seduced him. I was the tempter.[1]

Agnes Grey is not utterly corrupted by her experiences first at Wellwood and then Horton; but we are shown they do set fair to wreck her life. In a girl who started out guileless, ingenuous and open-minded, they have induced a sense of human incompetence and insufficiency that all but precludes marriage for her.

The author may here be writing very much from the heart. Of the three surviving Brontë sisters the various contemporary testimony has concurred with the view that Anne was the pretty one; she was personable and appealing as Charlotte, all self-consciously, was not. But if you are convinced you are unattractive—and in ways not only bodily—if you deem yourself unnoticeable and unmarriageable, unmarried is how you will tend to stay. It is really the function not of a look in a mirror which reveals actual deformity and repulsiveness: rather, a social and psychological disablement. And it is self-fulfilling. All compliment, all awakening interest in another party will appear mere vapour to you, will receive no appropriate response; indeed it will be repressed, stillborn, even in its very conception (within other people's awareness of you) by your habitual deportment, and paralysing self-estimate.

We the readers can see that Edward Weston is doing something not certainly but potentially 'speaking', in plucking those flowers for Miss Grey, but the latent significance of that gesture (not yet articulate for either of them, no doubt) the object of his attention misses: and the full text of her self-denigration we get in Chapter 17, concluding with this:

They that have beauty, let them be thankful for it, and make a good use of it, like any other talent; they that have it not, let them console themselves, and do the best they can without it: certainly, though liable to be over-estimated, it is a gift of God, and not to be despised. Many will feel this who have felt that they could love, and whose hearts tell them that they are worthy to be loved again; while yet they are debarred by the lack of this or some such seeming trifle, from giving and receiving that happiness they seem almost made to feel and to impart.

The primroses episode is as subtly handled as it needs to be. We should not respect Agnes if she were the sort of woman who saw flirtation in every male smile and a marriage proposal round every corner: that itself would betoken psychological disablement of a less attractive kind. And indeed the little scene *is* variously interpretable. Weston may simply help her pick her flowers out of politeness, or speak with her motivated by charity towards someone he recognizes as humanly very cut off and lonely; any sort of amorous implication is not—and should not be—explicit between them. For such a thing to be raised to the level of consciousness at all in either breast would signalize a crudity of response each to the other which would make them lesser people than they are.

What Anne Brontë is delineating with beautiful delicacy is one of those moments when someone may or may not be feeling his/her way toward you (in the sense of a more special relationship than good neighbourliness) and with a feeling the character of which they themselves have by no means analytically grasped; which the well-integrated person, when mutually disposed, will accept—i.e. *leave*—at that, to ride upon the air with its own vibration.

Locked by the behaviour of her successive households of employment, however, into a steep fall of self-confidence, Agnes Grey responds to Edward Weston's every word and gesture in a manner that would choke off interest in all but the most tenacious of suitors. On her side she keeps hoping for his attachment but has lost, because she has been discouraged from ever gaining, the social aplomb (i.e. through self-confidence) to ripen another's attention into regard and regard into courtship—which entails permitting, not hastening nor retarding, a process of self-confidence in the other party. All this is implicit in the inadequacy of her account of the business: 'It was Mr. Weston, of course—who else would trouble himself to do so much for *me*?'

Most of the time she is gauche in his company, we see, and speaks so much at cross-purposes as even to fail of giving her admirer knowledge of her new address in the coastal town where she and her mother are to set up their school when she leaves Horton.

All this is the more satisfactorily handled, in an artistic point of view, for not being explicit between author and reader—throughout. It is quietly intimated to us, but totally adumbrated, how this young couple come near to missing their best fulfilment in life on account of the sheer quantity of discouragement which, unawares, the heroine places in the hero's track: a misdirection itself born of *her* discouragement. And that that is to be laid at the door of the people with whom she has worked is illustrated most flagrantly when the Murray girls keep their instructress indoors and, in their meetings with Weston, allege she stays there by choice:

> 'And he asked after you again,' said Matilda, in spite of her sister's silent but imperative intimation that she should hold her tongue. 'He wondered why you were never with us, and thought you must have delicate health, as you came out so seldom.'
>
> 'He didn't, Matilda—what nonsense you're talking!'
>
> 'Oh, Rosalie, what a lie! He did, you know; and you said— Don't, Rosalie—hang it!—I won't be pinched so! And, Miss Grey, Rosalie told him you were quite well, but you were always so buried in your books that you had no pleasure in anything else!' (Ch. 17)

Rosalie Murray, not being emotionally inhibited, obviously *is* aware of the curate's potential devotion to her teacher and, wanting to engross all worthy male compliments in the district to herself, feigns lack of interest on the part of the one toward the other. It is very cruel and wrong, and *Agnes Grey*'s further substantiality as a portrait of life lies in anatomizing for us where such callousness derives.

In successive phases the two engagements its heroine takes on illustrate the origin and process of bad upbringing. The youngsters Agnes goes to are monsters of self-conceit and uncharitableness because they have been, and continue to be, parentally neglected. Basically their fathers and mothers do not care about them (as individuals); which is why they do not discipline them.

Chapter 3 demolishes all the modern cant about children being sacrosanct from bodily inflictions. Was there ever a gentler spirit than Anne Brontë's or her heroine's? Yet as Agnes is moved to protest:

> Master Tom, not content with refusing to be ruled, must needs set up as a ruler, and manifested a determination to keep, not only his sisters, but his governess in order, by violent manual and pedal applications; and, as he was a tall, strong boy of his years, this occasioned no trifling inconvenience. A few sound boxes in the ear, on such occasions, might have settled the matter easily enough: but as, in that case, he might make up some story to his mother, which she would be sure to believe, as she had such unshaken faith in his veracity—though I had already discovered it to be by no means unimpeachable—I determined to refrain from striking him, even in self-defence; and, in his most violent moods, my only resource was to throw him on his back, and hold his hands and feet till the frenzy was somewhat abated. To the difficulty of preventing him from doing what he ought not, was added that of forcing him to do what he ought. Often he would positively refuse to learn, or to repeat his lessons, or even to look at his book. Here, again, a good birch rod might have been serviceable; but, as my powers were so limited, I must make the best use of what I had.

For when all else fails the only thing which will speak to a morally deaf child is physical pain. Reasoning, civilized offered responses are unavailing because an alien language; and this in turn owing to the child's essential previous neglect.

Agnes Grey could not be more urgently relevant to our own society now: an age (as it seems to me) where perhaps most parents in all classes are in essentials just like the besotted Bloomfield and Murray adults. In too many cases nowadays folk appear to get married and have children, not for the love of those undertakings in themselves but as some sort of venture into additional human status, a further inward-looking *self*-endorsement. Mrs. Bloomfield is not interested in her offspring except as very tangential extensions of her own self-esteem and social aura: the hard work of a mother's love interests her not at all. That would involve effort, toil, care of a merely boring kind, because she is not in the first place bothered about having a *relationship* with her children. She wants them, but as items which can go in and out of some sort of cupboard in her life marked 'Progeny', and shut up there with a surrogate, the governess, who is officially employed to turn them into rational well-conducted creatures but who has hardly any real chance of doing so.

For the children, like all children, know when essentially they are minor tangentialities in their parents' values—always a ripe source of delinquency; and like all the cruelly indifferent, father and mother substitute a phoney humanitarianism in the place of true upbringing, as a sop to Cerberus and makeshift for the lapse on their part of the one thing needful, their attention.

Given that a majority of marriages and child-rearings are like this in the U.K. today (to judge by the theft endemic among 'middle' and 'upper'-class children, the pink and green hairstyles of the punk rockers—for what are these things but desperate cries for attention?) *Agnes Grey* can hardly be set aside as no tract for the times—our times.

The parents of 1983 are like the silly couples at Wellwood and Horton: they are wishful of anything for their children except to give them, consistently, out of a true devotion, their time, their interest, their selves: to bother with them. And then we wring our hands in adult colloquy about the rising crime wave of an affluent society and wonder how on earth atrocity can increase where social conditions are improved, historically, almost out of recognition. But children do not live by bread alone; they cope with life according as they are loved; which means being bothered with, related to, continually, by their progenitors and home-makers.

In the two youths who some months ago actually broke into the house of an old woman of 96 and raped her, we see the breakdown of even the most (one would have thought) funda-mental taboos of creaturely life; and without question they must have been subhuman to be able to do that. Yet what was even their act but a revenge upon the bad parenthood generally prevalent in our society? And a function of the rottenness of

26

that state, that primary tie, in our day is the general refusal, codified by the intelligentsia into a dogma, to have real discipline around, including corporal punishment, whether at home or at school. For as the devil Screwtape points out to his minion Wormwood:

> The use of Fashions in thought is to distract the attention of men from their real dangers. We direct the fashionable outcry of each generation against those vices of which it is least in danger and fix its approval on the virtue nearest to that vice which we are trying to make endemic. The game is to have them all running about with fire extinguishers whenever there is a flood, and all crowding to that side of the boat which is already nearly gunwale under. Thus we make it fashionable to expose the dangers of enthusiasm at the very moment when they are all really becoming worldly and lukewarm; a century later, when we are really making them all Byronic and drunk with emotion, the fashionable outcry is directed against the dangers of the mere 'understanding'. Cruel ages are put on their guard against Sentimentality, feckless and idle ones against Respectability, lecherous ones against Puritanism; and whenever all men are really hastening to be slaves or tyrants we make Liberalism the prime bogey.[2]

Exactly. In our epoch, when children's great predicament is that they are undisciplined (because ignored and unloved), the spectre which raises so very many teachers' and parents' hands in horror is the mere idea of corporal—indeed of any real—punishment.

Thus it is that both sets of parents can be so little aware of their offspring's true characters, can demand of Miss Grey that she turn them out as superior in behaviour to the hoydenism which at best, for instance, the girls display; and yet be affronted at any suggestion of bit or curb in a coherent process of character-training (*viz.* Mrs. Murray's reproaches in Ch. 18).

Hence it is that Tom Bloomfield can be so hideously cruel to animals, and his siblings with him (Chs. 2 and 5), in scenes which have provoked disbelief. Much that we pride our humanity upon are virtues and reciprocities acquired, by no means guaranteed as birthright for the species; and *homo sapiens* tends to love and care for living things only as he knows

27

love and care experientially himself. When children are brought into the world by begetters who are not interested in them—when they are denied the primary experience of love so completely as *that*—how will they have 'natural' feelings towards plants, the animal kingdom or their own kind?

Anne Brontë, in Chapters 21 and 22, sends her heroine to stay with the young married Rosalie Murray within a year of her becoming a lady of the manor at Ashby Park, not simply to fill out her story, nor to exhibit supernatural piety in forgiveness and charitable feeling on the observant governess's part towards a former tormentor; but to trace into a new generation yet again the consequences of this sort of denial which was prevalent amongst the higher classes in her day and which—perhaps with so much relative prosperity materially—has now spread through our society as a whole.

What Agnes discovers in that brief cheerless visit is not merely, as expected, that Rosalie does not care for her husband, is already at enmity with his family and something of a prisoner in the round of her rural wedded condition—*because* there is so little real affection and respect on both sides of a marriage made from paltry motives. The new mother cannot even love her child, and has just the same disparaging dismissive feelings about the baby to whom she herself has given birth that were all she really inspired in her own parent:

'But I can't devote myself entirely to a child,' said she: 'it may die—which is not at all improbable.'

'But, with care, many a delicate infant has become a strong man or woman.'

'But it may grow so intolerably like its father that I shall hate it.'

'That is not likely; it is a little girl, and strongly resembles its mother.'

'No matter; I should like it better if it were a boy—only that its father will leave it no inheritance that he can possibly squander away. What pleasure can I have in seeing a girl grow up to eclipse me, and enjoy those pleasures that I am for ever debarred from? But supposing I could be so generous as to take delight in this, still it is *only* a child; and I can't centre all my hopes in a child: that is only one degree better than devoting oneself to a dog. And as for all the wisdom and goodness you

28

have been trying to instil into me—that is all very right and proper I dare say, and if I were some twenty years older, I might fructify by it: but people must enjoy themselves when they are young; and if others won't let them—why, they must hate them for it!'

Egotism in its turn will no doubt be the psychological portion of a child so raised; and that self-conceit disables others who are not even guilty of being blood-kindred is what the previous chapters of the novel have shown, with the assault on the governess's capacity for happiness made by her ordeal in both her situations of employment. Her experience of the outer world, after a sheltered childhood, proves to be of an arena where people look over or through her and withhold all sense of her having a human value; so she all but becomes unmarriage-able. Philip Larkin has put it memorably:

> Man hands on misery to man.
> It deepens like a coastal shelf.[3]

and Anne Brontë is here tracing the process in its origins.

Agnes Grey, then, is about the way all of us tend to mutilate one another's lives—radically—in affording our fellow creatures less than full respect as equal beings having an independent importance like to our own: which is as much as to say, the manner to some degree most of us treat each other most of the time.

The novel is also about coping, however; about making something workable out of the human mess. Its heroine achieves this in virtue of her moral education in a loving environment, her training and religious piety from a background of fine sensibility—and the randomness of life itself.

She starts with supplemental advantages that may by no means be underived. Her imagination and the sly humour which animates a considerable portion of her narrative them-selves constitute a resilience under the pressures all around. Take the following, for example, concerning the senior Mrs. Bloomfield:

> Hitherto, though I saw the old lady had her defects (of which one was a proneness to proclaim her perfections), I had always

been wishful to excuse them, and to give her credit for all the virtues she professed, and even imagine others yet untold. (Ch. 4)

It is the subtlety of the final nuance there which invigorates— as it is indeed the function of a vigour in the writer. That sentence is a straightforward, obvious enough piece of satire until its last clause briefly makes us skid. There the hyperbole of feeling is shown in the context to have several constituents. The young woman is desperately lonely and clutching at straws:

> Kindness, which had been the food of my life through so many years, had lately been so entirely denied me, that I welcomed with grateful joy the slightest semblance of it.

She is also setting up as a judicious judge, self-consciously slightly witty, though we cannot forget she is only 19. The tone is of a self-possession and social ease which are not really secure, and yet which is the honest property of a genuinely discriminative mind.

It is the ability to transmit trace-elements of this sort of light weight yet significance which made me before think of Jane Austen and Professor George Whalley's words on that novelist's 'delight in effortless virtuosity, in catching by an impossible fraction of a hair's-breadth the savour of a nuance of implication'.[4]

This is not the leading hallmark of Agnes Grey's mind and rhetoric; Anne Brontë's themes are different. Yet the capacity to mock the old lady, mock herself and make several serious points with the necessary fugitiveness that characteristically we find here, itself represents a human value which is also a defence—however much that is to be seen as more securely acquired in retrospect than at the time.

Or we can turn to Chapter 19. Here a less qualified kind of irony operates which signifies a very amiable robustness in the moral nature of the bereaved family that the surviving Grey womenfolk have now become:

> 'Your grandpapa has been so kind as to write to me. He says he has no doubt I have long repented of my "unfortunate marriage," and if I will only acknowledge this, and confess I was wrong in neglecting his advice, and that I have justly suffered for it, he

will make a lady of me once again—if that be possible after my long degradation—and remember my girls in his will.'

But Mrs. Grey intends to answer with defiance and specifies the various heads of her reasoning why, concluding

'Will this do, children?—or shall I say we are all very sorry for what has happened during the last thirty years, and my daughters wish they had never been born; but since they have had that misfortune, they will be thankful for any trifle their grandpapa will be kind enough to bestow?'

Of course, we both applauded our mother's resolution; Mary cleared away the breakfast things; I brought the desk; the letter was quickly written and despatched; and, from that day, we heard no more of our grandfather, till we saw his death announced in the newspaper a considerable time after—all his worldly possessions, of course, being left to our wealthy, unknown cousins.

A word *en passant* here. Does not *Agnes Grey* very considerably more than any other Brontë novel stick to the sort of realism which Charlotte Brontë sought to infuse into the nineteenth century's fiction at the commencement of *her* public foray?[5]

Finally, in proof of our heroine's vitality as a centre of discriminations we have her ear for dialogue. Anyone who can reproduce as faithfully as she does very different styles of speech, sometimes in proximity together, and even the variations of an individual's modes of discourse, has by definition an extrovert awareness of others and life's variety which itself confers hope upon her fate as well as facilitating an active conscience.

'I have another place to go to,' said he, 'and I see' (glancing at the book on the table) 'some one else has been reading to you.'

'Yes, sir; Miss Grey has been as kind as to read me a chapter; an' now she's helping me with a shirt for our Bill but I'm feared she'll be cold there. Won't you come to th'fire, miss?'. . .

'Miss Grey,' said he half-jestingly, as if he felt it necessary to change the present subject, whether he had anything particular to say or not, 'I wish you would make my peace with the squire, when you see him. He was by when I rescued Nancy's cat, and did not quite approve of the deed. I told him I thought he might better spare all his rabbits than she her cat, for which audacious assertion he treated me to some rather ungentlemanly language;

and I fear I retorted a trifle too warmly.'

'Oh, lawful sir! I hope you didn't fall out wi' th' maister for sake o' my cat! he cannot bide answering again—can th' maister.'

'Oh, it's no matter, Nancy: I don't care about it, really; I said nothing *very* uncivil; and I suppose Mr. Murray is accustomed to use rather strong language when he's heated.' (Ch. 12)

The slight orotund pomposity of language, the relatively elaborate grammatical organization in the longest sentence there quoted contrasts with the other remarks Mr. Weston makes to his two parishioners. He is embarrassed both at the context and content of what he finds to say at that juncture and his diction subtly alters, accordingly.

The use and aid of such equipment for an ethical being has already been shown in the way Agnes reports her tearful self-pity and maudlin self-contempt during the primroses episode: 'Such a discovery would make my eyes gush out with water, no doubt; but that was one of my greatest enjoyments now.' The self-indulgence is there contained and disciplined by a conscience, we realize, habituated to exercise and examination.

Starch of a more nutritive kind is supplied by her religion. Ultimately she has not been brought up to expect, i.e. demand, of this world a nice time. (Osip Mandelstam's words to his wife, before dying for his brave outspokenness, put the matter at its most bleakly direct: 'Why do you think you ought to be happy?') Indeed the more I study Anne Brontë's work the more it seems to me she is first and foremost a Christian writer; and this creates problems in connection with a late-twentieth-century readership at least analogous to the question of the validity, for our society now, of Europe's medieval poetry, shot through as most of that is with a religious interpretation of existence. The issue is so large I choose to try and take the bull by the horns in a separate section later. Suffice it to say here it is significant that Anne Brontë, as was remarked before, accomplishes the most 'realistic' story of any fiction the Haworth sisters chose to publish. *Agnes Grey* has no unanswered questions like the method of Heathcliff's making his fortune before he returns to Wuthering Heights, or *Jane Eyre* with its magnificent psychology yet preposterous plot.

It rides beautifully between the Scylla and Charybdis of any social realist in the form. On the one side, it does not yield to softness: in E. M. Forster's words, 'the temptation's overwhelming to grant to one's creations a happiness actual life does not supply.'[6] On the other hand, it does not flog its characters with a grim Hardyesque determinism of misery, something no less fantastic, at least in its artistic effect. The Brontës' actual life-history reads fully as unfortunate as *Jude the Obscure*'s, but were it hawked in a fiction we should probably withhold credence. The trouble with Hardy for me is that, like real life sometimes (as Forster has elsewhere also remarked), he 'gets things wrong',[7] and the awful trajectories of his heroes' courses all but overwhelm the other, wonderful features of his prose writing because they create the impression of an universe deliberately malign without 'arguing the case', imaginatively speaking, for such a view; sufficiently at least to carry conviction during the space of the reading. 'Yet *why* are these people so remarkably stupid and dogged by such unusual quantities of stupendous ill-luck?' is my repeated moan as I trace the agonies of Jude and his fellow-sufferers. 'If "It", as Goldsworthy Lowes Dickinson called the First Cause, were so implacably cruel, surely the first amoeba would never have managed to crawl out of the slime.'

I *think* the complaint has little to do with the portion of tragedies in one's own life. Different authors can penetrate us with the sense, at least for the nonce, that 'not to be born is best' or, in C. S. Lewis's words immediately after the death of his wife, trying out the voice of *advocatus diaboli* 'Fate (or whatever it is) delights to produce a great capacity and then frustrate it. Beethoven went deaf. By our standards a mean joke; the monkey trick of a spiteful imbecile.'[8] But they do so, these other writers, by means more solidly based and inwardly structured.

Agnes Grey suffers enough and various afflictions to become representative of ordinary humanity—equally in the lower-to-middle middle classes of her day, and at large. Her home life is happy at first, but her father loses his money and by the standards of their caste their means become almost desperately straitened; and the psychological as well as material costs of this débâcle are registered. She sets out to earn her own living and add something to the common funds besides, by teaching; and finds the task not only unpleasant but degrading—not once but twice over. Her sister marries, modestly. Her mother becomes a widow, and when they set up a school together they have to work hard to make ends meet with no provision in view should either of them be stricken ill, except that of falling hard upon her brother-in-law and *his* thin means. Agnes loves, but her affection seems unrequited and she has to reconcile herself to the nearly certain prospect of a future as a hapless old maid.

This constitutes a sufficient series of possibilities followed up by frustrations. More would look like authorial obtuseness. We should say in that case, 'Well if life is really tougher still than this—more painful, of its own intrinsic logic, *inevitably*— it is hardly worth caring about in the first place. With the words of Ernest Hemingway's heroine at the end of *A Farewell to Arms*, "It's just a dirty trick" (Ch. 41), our most appropriate response would be to turn our faces thankfully to the wall whenever we could and like her expire with an expression of contempt upon them.' On the other hand, if Agnes Grey's career were pleasanter we should be tempted to retort, 'Very nice, but where have all the bereavements and economic hardships gone, the frustrations intellectual and emotional? There seem to be plenty more of such things in the world outside than between the covers of this book. It's just a novelette of female wish-fulfilment.'

In short, it appears to me Anne Brontë pitches the matter just right. The duplication of unsatisfactory households in which her heroine works makes a social criticism even as it builds the picture of a whole social world. The upper classes in her time have too much power, too much freedom to be bad. That they use these liberties ill is thoroughly exemplified, not only by the characters of the Bloomfields and the Murrays and their on the whole repulsive children, but by the local squire-archies in each case surrounding them and their various relations and friends.

This is the book's Tyranny-theme in its political aspect: that in such a society as early Victorian Britain, certain individuals can disregard too many aspects of the Golden Rule just because they have lots of money. It is all-significant that more than one type of gentry abuses equally their freedoms of cash and time: Mr. Bloomfield the self-made tradesman, Mr. Murray of the 'genuine thoroughbred gentry' (Ch. 6) and the lower aristocracy with whom he associates. The implication of this is evident for us, though never worked out or otherwise than implicit in the text: the need so to restructure society's economics that one group does not exist in a state of nearly complete possession and others in almost total dependence. And indeed upon the same theme the British nation has exercised itself more impressively than most other communities, historically considered, during the past century and a half.

Terry Eagleton, writing from a Marxist point of view, offers generous appreciation of certain features of Anne Brontë in general and the present work in particular. E.g.,

> Whereas Lucy Snowe's chiding of Polly Home and Ginevra Fanshawe betrays less reputable motives than mere moral disinterestedness, Agnes Grey admonishes her obnoxious charges with a remarkable freedom from personal malice—the more remarkable because we have in this work a more direct and detailed account of the social violence to which the governess is subjected than anything we find elsewhere in the Brontës.[9]

Noting that 'Her fraught relation to her pupils . . . provides a painfully lucid image of "genteel" poverty's unwilling alliance with morally irresponsible wealth',[10] he accurately indicates *why* 'Agnes's responses are cooler, more equable than those we find in a Charlotte protagonist's truck with the gentry'; it is because here the heroine's 'own *amour-propre* is not fundamentally at stake'.

He declares also that she and the book avoid smugness. He confesses its lucidity:

> Its final line—'And now I think I have said sufficient'—neatly captures the laconic modesty of the whole, the sense of a work attractively reserved in feeling without any loss of candid revelation.[11]

Yet ultimately, he argues, 'the orthodox critical judgement that Anne Brontë's work is slighter than her sisters' is just',[12] because there is only 'one brief moment in *Agnes Grey* when

Agnes, dispirited by her fruitless efforts to instil moral principle into the Murrays' spoilt brats, wonders whether her own standards of rectitude might not be insidiously eroded by daily contact with such dissoluteness.'[13] Always in her work there is a 'partial unhinging of the "moral" from a nurturing social context'.[14]

But such a complaint is more about the novel's subject-matter than its treatment thereof. For the predicament, how to be a relatively responsible moral agent and cope with inhabiting a delinquent social world, when life itself also offers plenty of frustrations, is one in which every decent reader of the book must be interested. Anne Brontë does not (*pace* Dr. Eagleton) oppose the 'social' and the 'moral': that primroses episode alone, to which I keep referring simply as a type of the whole, showed us the governess's feelings on being not recognized by society as a full human entity not only being analysed by her; they were presented (by the author which notionally she has become) as more complex, fraught and vulnerable—the tone does this, the juxtaposition of events in the passage quoted—than she herself recognized at the time. She is more pained and compromised than she admits. That is what we are made and given to see, exemplified as it is by the way a certain literariness will rub shoulders uneasily with more direct colloquial narrative: 'I presently fell back, and began to botanise and entomologise . . .'. We realize that she does not entirely know any longer how to manage her self-awareness while yet being conscious that it is perilously near to sentimental self-pity.

Her religious convictions and training preserve her however, we can see, from progressive mere self-endorsement and ultimately cranky isolation. They save her from a collapse of the self, in giving an exterior standard—the Gospels' hopes and commands—by which to keep measuring her conduct and attitudes. Faced with the lapse, pretty well, of her hope of marriage and doomed, as it appears, to a future of worthiness but boredom, she articulates this:

> Should I shrink from the work that God had set before me, because it was not fitted to my taste? Did not He know best what I should do, and where I ought to labour? and should I

long to quit His service before I had finished my task, and expect to enter His rest without having laboured to earn it? (Ch. 21)

Nor is it that she strikes us, on such occasions, as some haloed goody-goody, in her commitment to the 'strait gate and narrow way': she can show the refreshing fierceness of the truly, likeably virtuous from time to time, when appropriately provoked. Writing of Mr. Robson's encouragement of his nephew Tom Bloomfield's 'propensity to persecute the lower creation, both by precept and example', we have the following:

> As he frequently came to course or shoot over his brother-in-law's grounds, he would bring his favourite dogs with him; and he treated them so brutally that, poor as I was, I would have given a sovereign any day to see one of them bite him, provided the animal could have done it with impunity. (Ch. 5)

Significantly it is when she has resigned herself, *actively*, to her lot—a worthy one as an instructress in the seminary of her own making but a fate without joy—that the break comes. *Agnes Grey* illustrates thus the Christian gloss upon Elizabeth Bowen's great dictum, 'We are constructed for full living. Occasion rarely offers'; and E. M. Forster's apt comment in *A Passage to India*, 'Adventures do occur, but not punctually.'

'Unless the grain dies. . . .' Only when the heart has resigned its earthly hopes (especially its very dearest ones) in favour of obedience to its supreme marriage-bond, its role as Bride of the Lamb, can God afford to make this-worldly happiness available to those He loves as children who *can* be saved. Until then, awarding us the felicities we ache, the reliefs we gasp for, as the central fulfilments in our lives, He is just encouraging us to dance off down a mirage-track to ultimate death beside the transitory water-holes of our own imaging.

After plenty of happy upbringing, followed by oppression and suppression, Agnes has to lose her last great hope this side of the grave—beyond that of doing her duty as a Christian—and she has to live on quite a while with that lost hope rendered seemingly permanent as lost; before its realization arrives after all.

*   *   *

When it does so, Prince Charming hardly sweeps her off in a glass coach at one bound, nor with brightly caparisoned chargers. Edward Weston's situation and character are perfect for the book's purposes. He is sturdy and real enough to be reassuring: no mere cardboard cut-out of a perfect cleric with extremely modest means. Yet he is intrinsically un-exciting enough to figure in the reader's lay-mind as not—like marriage to Mr. Darcy for Elizabeth Bennet in *Pride and Prejudice*—a brilliant upshot for the heroine's career, both socially and emotionally. After their re-encounter by happy chance (here Life's own helpful randomness comes in) on the sands of Agnes's new home town, it takes some time before he proposes marriage, some weeks indeed—and then the romance is very quiet. Winifred Gérin has censured the close of the novel as exposing interests uncombined, not unified, on the author's part:

> Yet it was inevitable that the dual purpose of the book should emerge; that those portions which were derived from fact should be more vividly realised and that the purely fictitious incidents should be slurred over, as inappropriate, as it were, to the fuller treatment. Thus the happy ending to which, as fiction, Anne had not the heart to deny her heroine, is written in so low and subdued a key that it saddens rather than elates the reader. Judged from the standpoint of art this is a mistake; the story of *Agnes Grey* begun in such buoyant style, with so much wit and sparkle, should not modulate into a minor key and close in solemnity since, in spite of some tribulations, the heroine's happiness is assured.[15]

But that misses the various points of which the accomplishment is here achieved. (1) The book is about the business of reconciling oneself to possible modes of happiness, not extremely unlikely ones—as well as to actual species of suffering. Were the hero handsome, witty, rich and charming, we should ignore the whole as a day-dream: for how often could portionless young governesses, gauche of manner and no brilliant beauties withal, get proposals from such as they—then or now? (2) It helps solve the aesthetic problem for most novels with a happy ending—the suggestion, artistically constituted by the very *procédé* of the plot, that life has now stopped, albeit on a plateau of fulfilments. We cannot imagine

Elizabeth and Darcy living through their first married quarrel
or the death of a child; rightly—we do not want to and there
would be no value in the exercise. It would be a 'How many
children had Lady Macbeth?' sort of question. But here it is of
the essence of the piece, our well knowing that trials face the
couple of the concluding scene—several of these in his pastoral
life and her parish-work at Horton we have beheld already. Life
carries on at the close of *Agnes Grey* and it is the real life where *'il
faut cultiver son jardin'*. If the young pair do not attempt to
penetrate the aristocracy nor hold themselves entirely aloof
from it but keep fairly distant from certain classes' routines and
blandishments with no sense of loss, it is in order to stay
'unspotted from the World' in the sense that we associate that
term with 'the Flesh and the Devil'. This is no question of
retreat or escapism, quite the reverse. We see two committed
social workers taking up their task in the broad blaze of
historical day and the middle of public highways at the end of
Anne Brontë's first novel. Miss Grey's fate, far from being a sort
of transcendent one, untied to the earth, like the brides' at the
ends of most comedy, means happiness; but happiness in the
world outside the covers of a human celebration, and amidst
that world's problems.

What could be set down for a flaw is the book's failure to
convey the lovers' feelings for each other, or at least its heroine's
for its hero, from the inside in their full 'romantic' aspect. This is
a *manque* writ larger in *The Tenant of Wildfell Hall*. In both works
we know that the characters have powerful amorous inclinations towards each other: but as a Briton and an Australian are
well aware that their respective countries exist on opposite
shores of the globe without appreciating those terrains in their
reality until they have paid a visit the one to the other. When
not only Helen Graham's response to Arthur Huntingdon, in
the early time of their acquaintance, is mediated to us *sans* its
full alleged erotic colouring and necessary emotional intensity,
but also Huntingdon's later for Annabella Lowborough and,
here, Agnes Grey's for Edward Weston, we are likely to suspect
that some sort of psychological inhibition was operative in this
author—perhaps an excess of delicacy. But we must also
appreciate that conveying passion is no facile undertaking,
artistically considered. Henry James was surely a born novelist

if ever there has been one, and his pages throb with the sexual interest woken by men and women in each other: *The Awkward Age* seems to me white hot, like poor Nanda Brookenham's face there, with the passion of her feeling for Vanderbank. But it is not till as late in his career as *The Golden Bowl* (1905) that James can make his characters convincingly embrace, and had he died at the same early age as Anne Brontë (he would have been 29 years and 4 months old in August 1872) what would he have left to show of *his* excellent craftsmanship, his true novelistic gift and inspiration? Well, one novel *Watch and Ward* (1869); nineteen tales, up to 'Guest's Confession'; and some substantial travel and critical writings—but no such masterwork as *A Portrait of a Lady*.

While this is a flaw in *The Tenant* and a serious one, we may even vindicate it in *Agnes Grey*, the unsubstantiated *inner* life of the lovers' feelings for each other; since throughout the whole, Weston is seen, necessarily for the novel's effect, *ab exteriori* (being registered through the anxious uncertain eyes of the governess), and the tale concludes with the relief of her emotions in his proposal, a rescue and fulfilment about which it would be tasteless in her to brag.

That their religious commitment has its own dangers Anne Brontë is also concerned to illustrate. In the case of old Nancy Brown (Ch. 11, 'The Cottagers') she shows the religious melancholy infused into nineteenth-century life in consequence of the Evangelical Movement and its reanimation of a living Church in her society. This elderly widow is harrowed by the very creed which ought to comfort her:

> '. . . th' prayer-book only served to show me how wicked I was, that I could read such good words an' never be no better for it, and oftens feel it a sore labour an' a heavy task beside, instead of a blessing and a privilege as all good Christians does. It seemed like as all were barren an' dark to me. And then, them dreadful words, "Many shall seek to enter in, and shall not be able." They like as they fair dried up my sperrit.'

With this instance Anne Brontë is not only working out a major quarrel with herself—there is little evidence to contradict the view of both her sister Charlotte and her biographer that it was in battling against religious melancholy that most of her own brief life was spent—she is 'being fair' as a creative spirit and implying, with exemplary equity, how the very philosophy she commends to society carries, like any doctrine which is a reading of History and an ethos, its own pitfalls too:

> '. . . I tried to do my duty as aforetime: but I like got no peace. An' I even took the sacrament; but I felt as though I were eating and drinking to my own damnation all th' time. So I went home, sorely troubled.'

As well as the moral strengthening and psychic power, for the individual and the community, deriving from Christian conviction, there will be casualties who need aid.

Aid may come in the form of direct sensible and perceptive pastoral counsel. Mr Weston the new curate points out that we love by practice; in acting out a pretence of the Saviour's commands, our habits become reality, the Beast behind the beautiful mask becomes a Beauty.

> 'But if you cannot feel positive affection for those who do not care for you, you can at least try to do to them as you would they should do unto you: you can endeavour to pity their failings and excuse their offences, and to do all the good you can to those about you. And if you accustom yourself to this, Nancy, the very effort itself will make you love them in some degree— to say nothing of the goodwill your kindness would beget in them, though they might have little else that is good about them. . . .' (Ch. 11)

Divine counsel will also be available, advice not made with hands or uttered by human voices—in the grandeur, the elevating loveliness of Nature. A kind of *basso ostinato* runs through this book as through all of Anne Brontë's work, a first-hand experience of Nature as restorative, invigorating, a spiritual sanctuary and very present help in trouble. Again and again the heroine is struck by some prospect or deliberately goes to feed upon some part of the physical environment which encompasses mere men, finding there new strength and fresh comfort.

> And then, the unspeakable purity and freshness of the air! there was just enough heat to enhance the value of the breeze, and just enough wind to keep the whole sea in motion, to make the

> waves come bounding to the shore, foaming and sparkling, as if
> wild with glee. Nothing else was stirring—no living creature
> was visible besides myself. My footsteps were the first to press
> the firm, unbroken sands;—nothing before had trampled them
> since last night's flowing tide had obliterated the deepest marks
> of yesterday, and left it fair and even, except where the sub-
> siding water had left behind it the traces of dimpled pools, and
> little running streams. (Ch. 24)

Hence the appositeness of her meeting Weston again, after
thinking perpetually to have lost him, upon these sands of 'A-'.
She has come to drink once more at the only fount where such
perceptions and thirsts as (say) Wordsworth's could be slaked;
and in doing so for its own sake has had everything else she
cares for added unto her.

Which makes another point. Good Chance also exists. That
too is part of God's Creation, the reality with which we
humans have to come to terms. Weston may well be suspected
of having accepted a living near 'A-' in the hope of one day
running into his heart's best find. He has helped, if we will,
give Luck a nudge, even a hearty one. But now he and his
bride-to-be have been assisted by the randomness of things as
well as hindered, in the past, by their cruelty: here it has
expressed itself in his being offered such a living as 'F-', 'a
village about two miles distant', in the first place; and in the
second, their re-encountering as they do.

Nevertheless there *is* an aspect in which the story is con-
summated with a sense of anti-climax. Miss Gérin has the
right idea by the wrong end. Similarly to Colonel Brandon in
Sense and Sensibility, though with rather more individualized
character, Agnes Grey's lover constitutes no thrilling human
presence; and we wish wistfully that he did.

But then by what right should he? Like most of us, the
governess herself, considered whether physically or morally,
socially or intellectually, is not the catch of catches. Yet she
has a passionate yearning heart and the instinctual wisdom to
fix upon what it can elevate to absolute value *by its very devotion*.
Thus much we deduce, I think, across the trajectory of her
rhetoric. For as Metropolitan Anthony Bloom once pointed
out,[16] it is the character of Love to make significant what is
even of itself trivial. And Weston is far more than that.

'Agnes Grey': Accommodating Reality

It is questionable all the same whether Agnes could so elevate a man like Mr. Hatfield, Horton's worldly vicar, or some member of Rosalie Murray's set of squirearchical-aristocratic admirers, even if she were noticed by them. They lack a dimension of conscience and feeling necessary to give those responses which can make Love a prosperous horticulturist. Her marriage with the former curate however can *become* something great (we again intuit), though he is not the most exciting individual since Sir Philip Sidney. She has herself planted half the garden her devotion will raise in the soil of this man's worthiness, somewhat stolid as it is. But that won't make its fruits and blooms any less real or precious than they already promise to be.

All this shows as mattering the more in the context of a novel which has illustrated only too vividly through most of its course what people are like when morally untutored by either precept or suffering.

The subject-matter and style of this book are of the first importance—in their very quietness. In a sense Anne Brontë's relegation is the final proof of her success. Her compact but richly realized fable about what life is like and how to live works so totally, it is eclipsed by fierier rockets of illumination that throw a more fitful glare upon the scene. *Agnes Grey* is full of the way in which people have to make ends meet—financially, psychologically—in the real world; and Life's own creative play there as well.

NOTES

1. Op. cit., Fontana edition (London, 1967), p. 26.
2. *The Screwtape Letters* (London, 1942), pp. 128–29.
3. *High Windows* (London, 1974), p. 30.
4. In *Jane Austen's Achievement*, ed. Juliet McMaster (London, 1976), pp. 121–22.
5. 'By the time she wrote [*The Professor*] her taste and judgment had revolted against the exaggerated idealisms of her early girlhood, and she went to the extreme of reality, closely depicting characters as they had

43

shown themselves to her in actual life: if there they were strong even to coarseness—as was the case with some that she had met with in flesh-and-blood existence—she "wrote them down an ass;" if the scenery of such life as she saw was for the most part wild and grotesque, instead of pleasant or picturesque, she described it line for line. The grace of the one or two scenes and characters which are drawn rather from her own imagination than from absolute fact, stand out in exquisite relief from the deep shadows and wayward lines of others, which call to mind some of the portraits of Rembrandt.'—Mrs. Gaskell's *Life* (ed. Ward & Shorter), p. 313.

6. E. M. Forster, *Maurice* (London, 1971): quoted in P. N. Furbank's Introduction, letter to G. L. Dickinson of 13 December 1914.
7. *Abinger Harvest* (pocket edn., London 1940), from 1932 review of Jane Austen's Letters, p. 158.
8. *A Grief Observed* (London, 1961), section II, para. 1.
9. Terry Eagleton, *Myths of Power: A Marxist Study of the Brontës* (London, 1975), p. 123.
10. Ibid., p. 124. The quote immediately following in my text is from this page also.
11. Ibid., p. 126.
12. Ibid., p. 134.
13. Ibid., p. 123.
14. Ibid., p. 132.
15. W. Gérin, *Anne Brontë* (London [1959]; rev. edn., 1976), p. 230.
16. At a religious meeting-and-discussion session in York University, *circa* 1978.

2

The Poems

Reading Anne Brontë's poetry is a peculiar activity. We are in presence of a first-hand experience of Nature and an authentic religious outlook, mediated to us, like her sister Emily's verse, by language-processes that are not quite (in the main) sufficient. Just as Emily Brontë ought to rank with Blake for her visionary lyrics, so Anne Brontë would enjoy Emily Dickinson's status, we recurrently are inclined to feel, if only their literary means had been slightly better adapted to the calibre of their inspiration.

Anne's last poem 'A dreadful darkness closes in' (written 7 to 28 January 1849 in face of her fatal illness; pp. 163–64 of Chitham's edition) perfectly exemplifies this. It has all sorts of power; of kinds we associate with Dickinson's name—and George Herbert. The sixteen four-line stanzas written in the fashion of a hymn, which to some extent they are, yet intense, personalized in a way that makes it less than wholly suitable for public acts of worship, are just one aspect of this kinship, condensing as they do an anguish, a struggle into deliberately disciplined and formalized utterance of which the very restraint testifies to the speaker's suffering.

> But Thou hast fixed another part,
>   And Thou hast fixed it well;
> I said so with my breaking heart
>   When first the anguish fell. (ll. 21–4)

'Well' in line 22 there would just make the thought mere whistling in the dark, a sort of spurious religiose claim to insight, but that what immediately follows acknowledges how

45

the struggle to think like this—implicit in fidelity to her Creed—is unceasing, is far from accomplished. The whole moreover is so poignantly actualized by the non-specificity of 'the anguish' at the close, transforming what would otherwise be an undistinguished verse. In not yet stipulating exactly what kind of agony has descended upon her the poet both intensifies and generalizes it. It does truly become a type of all pain-filled defeat, Everyman's; which is where indeed she is all but desperately seeking to locate it. To become bearable, her deprivation has to be seen in its character as part of every Christian pilgrim's progress; and it is only near the end that we realize that the grief at issue is not lost love, frustrated artistry, family bereavement or social ruin but the very near prospect of Death itself.

Her chosen form is likewise apt in presenting most of the stanzas as distilled and belaboured chunks of experience. The metric and rhyme scheme (8a 6b 8a 6b) and the brevity of the lines together offer the speaker's trouble as something recurrent, enclosed and enclosing, which has to be assailed again and again by the siege-engines of faith and obedience. Yet this effect is not overdone. Just when it would otherwise turn slightly monotonous into a hymnodic sing-song routine, Anne Brontë varies the rhythm (after line 36) and does not entirely restore the verse-measure to its original discipline till line 55, four and a half stanzas later; a procedure by which of course she achieves other things as well.

Weariness, too, is expressed by the poem's central method, presenting its matter as considerations that develop in sequence yet come somewhat separated off from one another. But not only weariness. Though the work moves with a voice of stumbling difficulty, yet it has an inner logic as an argument. Faced by the Fates' apparent sentence,

> A dreadful darkness closes in
>   On my bewildered mind;

the author asks for resignation in a right frame of thinking and lifts her aim to the fount and goal of her being. What she prays for is comfort in the original sense used severely by the New Testament of the Holy Spirit (as Comforter): strengthening to pass safely through an ordeal, rather than relief.

She then reviews her life and admits (as it were) that she has been taken at her word as a Christian devotee:

> I've begged to serve Thee heart and soul,
>   To sacrifice to Thee
> No niggard portion, but the whole
>   Of my identity.

This oblation is now, it grimly seems, to be all too thoroughly accepted; yet even as half-complaint forms itself a second time (lines 25–8, the first being implicit in 17–20), she confesses another unanswerable part of her theology:

> The hope and the delight were Thine;
>   I bless Thee for their loan;

she offers, God takes, only what is and always was His anyway; and His was always likewise all the happiness, all the motives to happiness, interest in living, virtue and value of existence, in the first place. He provided that to begin with. Further,

> I gave Thee while I deemed them mine
>   Too little thanks, I own.

It prompts her to still more fruit of logic and virtue:

> Shall I with joy Thy blessings share
>   And not endure their loss?
> Or hope the martyr's crown to wear
>   And cast away the cross?
>
> These weary hours will not be lost,
>   These days of passive misery,
> These nights of darkness anguish tost
>   If I can fix my heart on Thee.

Then the meditative process begins again which is at once suppressed and acknowledged lament against her evident destiny, and the tough determination to make the appointed *actual* lot tell for gain by living through it to a proper attitude.

The poem's kernel arrives at lines 51–2. Its ambition is 'To gather . . . holiness from woe'.

But the holiness has not yet, as it were finally and permanently, arrived. The penultimate stanza has a touch of

47

that attempt at bargain-driving which sometimes we find in the Bible: 'O let us live and we shall call upon thy Name' (Psalm 80, v. 18). A legitimate plea: in the case of the righteous king Hezekiah, after all, God granted it.

> If Thou shouldst bring me back to life
> More humbled I should be;
> More wise, more strengthened for the strife,
> More apt to lean on Thee.

We ought to remember here that the gentle, permanently convalescent and spotlessly resigned Anne of Brontë legend, a young woman whose early death was expected by her family all her life and who meekly awaited it on those terms, is largely mythopoeia, albeit of her sister's making. The true corrective gloss for this verse is her own magnificent letter from Haworth as late as 5 April 1849 to Ellen Nussey arguing for a change of scene the very next month:

> . . . But I have a more serious reason than this for my impatience of delay; the doctors say that change of air or removal to a better climate would hardly ever fail of success in consumptive cases if the remedy were taken in *time*, but the reason why there are so many disappointments is, that it is generally deferred till it is too late. Now I would not commit this error; and to say the truth, though I suffer much less from pain and fever than I did when you were with us, I am decidedly weaker and very much thinner, my cough still troubles me a good deal, especially in the night, and what seems worse than all I am subject to great shortness of breath on going up stairs or any slight exertion. Under these circumstances I think there is no time to be lost. I have no horror of death: if I thought it inevitable I think I could quietly resign myself to the prospect, in the hope that you, dear Miss Nussy [*sic*] would give as much of your company as you possibly could to Charlotte and be a sister to her in my stead. But I wish it would please God to spare me not only for Papa's and Charlotte's sakes, but because I long to do some good in the world before I leave it. I have many schemes in my head for future practise—humble and limited indeed—but still I should not like them to come to nothing, and myself to have lived to so little purpose. But God's will be done. . . .

This is not the language of one who assumes that her life ought to be brief.

Charlotte Brontë's report of both her sisters' actual demises as such is authoritative. But her account of their respective declines seems almost inverted (from whatever psychological cause or need on her own part) as to the moral truths deducible from the evidence. All the facts that survive testify not that Emily was 'torn from life' but rather conspired at her own end: the almost misanthropic way she spent her last full year of earthly existence—a selfhood withheld now at least from her female siblings in regard to sociability and compromise; the decline immediately following upon Branwell's death; the resolute resistance against all medical aid till it was hopeless at the very end. It is practically as if her life was bound up, by 1847, with her brother, not her sisters' and that once he perished she had nothing more to care for in this world. Alternatively, as Miss Gérin interprets the matter, in getting her to publish first her poetry and then *Wuthering Heights* (which received an uncomprehending press that of itself inflicted no small bitter draught) Charlotte had broken some magic spell, an essential spring in Emily's ability to relate to the world, to Nature and to herself.

Conversely, the view of Anne's delicate health which we have inherited is all Charlotte's as to its psychological reading. No doubt her relatives, always aware of Anne's delicacy, always feared for her the most. But that did not necessarily make life less precious to this particular possessor of it. We may well believe, not least on the evidence of this poem, that the sublime way in which she could, dying, impart strength to her companions—'Take courage!'—was something which had come after much struggle; as indeed is represented in the whole text presently under review. The last stanza simultaneously performs another of the reversions of mood that characterize the very predicament with which their victim is wrestling here—and enacts fulfilment of her initial prayer. She 'suffers but does not sin', because repining and mere grievance are definitively rejected. She is 'tortured yet resigned' at the close. This conclusion does not achieve a stasis of feeling, a plateau of now secured sanctity. The poem is much more impressive than that. It traces a recurrent process, the mind pacing round and round its new dreadful prison-cell but determined to pace creatively, in religious faithfulness, by appealing—by entirely turning and submitting—to God.

The whole poem has been hard-won and if ever anybody
wrote death-bed lines that deserve respect, these are they; so
that the two stanzas beginning

> I hoped amid the brave and strong
> My portioned task might lie,

have rightly passed into what in our fairly illiterate day
remains of the national poetic consciousness: not only as Anne
Brontë's key epitaph upon herself but as a classic embodiment
of vigorous resignation, of an energic and creative submission
to the Fates' decrees which all upright human beings will
aspire to possess for themselves.

Wherefore then do we not 'place' it with Marvell's 'Horatian
Ode' or the Holy Sonnets of John Donne?

I think the reason is, her language is not quite shocking
enough. Unnamed as it is, 'the anguish' transforms that sixth
stanza; but not all the verses are so altered by the slight jolts
which are required if this poem is to become a completely
great one. We constantly need a surprising novelty in the
speech amidst something formally so traditionalist as this
metric and the type of emotions it evokes; and such a charge
ultimately is to be preferred against all Anne Brontë's verses.

Comparison with the other poets I have named will illustrate
this. Here is Emily Dickinson in characteristic voice:

> There came a wind like a bugle;
> It quivered through the grass,
> And a green chill upon the heat
> So ominous did pass
> We barred the windows and the doors
> As from an emerald ghost;
> The doom's electric moccasin
> That very instant passed.
> On a strange mob of panting trees,
> And fences fled away,
> And rivers where the houses ran
> The living looked that day.
> The bell within the steeple wild
> The flying tidings whirled.
> How much can come
> And much can go,
> And yet abide the world!

It is not a voice wholly preferable, it is not William Shakespeare. She is a very exciting poet but much of the time, in the last analysis, she is too self-consciously poetic, there is just a little too much presence of the author in the text aware of her own gift for collocating in unusual ways words which are unlikely but apt partners. A lot of her work is a complete success, simply thrilling, but far more frequently than in (say) Milton we have a sense of the felicities of the speech being obtrusive, drawing attention to themselves. Nevertheless, it must be admitted we cannot imagine Anne Brontë striking out with 'The doom's electric moccasin'.

The sort of 'esemplasticity' of imagination in language there inherent is outside her range; which is a pity to the extent that something in that kind would be required fully to have made fresh and powerful the sorts of verse-forms Anne habitually chooses.

Likewise her poetry lacks the profundity that is to be found in an author not dissimilar as to ways and means and themes. George Herbert is superior because in a hymn-like stanza he surprises us not only as much as Emily Dickinson—linguistically yet without the self-consciousness—but also because he penetrates by very economic methods to deep profundities of thought:

> Love is swift of foote;
> Love's a man of warre,
>   And can shoot,
> And can hit from farre.

These, like all Herbert's best verse (and scarcely any of it is not 'best'—it is the finest religious poetry in English) are perfect truisms of Christian theology and feeling, axioms of European thought 1600 years old by the time they were printed. But they are united, those ideas, recombined in a slightly new and therefore startling perception. They have the same secret of poetic power, thus incarnated, that distinguishes Dante, whose greatest feature is not that he took upon himself to be a kind of Recording Angel (surely the least endearing characteristic of the *Divine Comedy* and one which ought to have come in for a lot more stick than it has won—especially from others professing and calling themselves Christians—

over the centuries) and damned alike historical personages and hostile contemporaries, but the utter simplicity of expression in him wherewith a profound concept is experienced afresh with new insight. An ancient known piece of doctrine, long consented to and made the philosophical wall-paper of our lives (love is good, hatred is bad, etc.) comes before us from a slightly different angle, viewed in a new and very illuminating collocation of first principles or metaphors. If we compare with these poets Anne Brontë's 'Music on Christmas Morning' (No. 27, pp. 96–7 in Chitham), we see her lack of such qualities at its most exposed. For example,

> With them I celebrate His birth—
> Glory to God in highest Heaven,
> Good-will to men, and peace on earth,
> To us a Saviour-king is given;
> Our God is come to claim His own,
> And Satan's power is overthrown!

Here the Christian doctrines are merely versified. Almost no new feeling animates them: in fact this is effectually acknowledged by the author in the italicizings of the next stanza:

> A sinless God, for sinful men,
> Descends to suffer and to bleed;
> Hell *must* renounce its empire then;
> The price is paid, the world is freed,
> And Satan's self must now confess
> That Christ has earned a *Right* to bless; . . .

It is not a matter of cosmological disputation to complain that this poem fails to point out what Dante or Herbert (no doubt rather breathtakingly) would have hinted at least: namely *why*. A Christian poet not even of their stature but (say) John Donne's would elucidate and embody the obligation in a paradox or conceit that itself, however daringly, actualized the compulsion—Satan's loss of his empire—here in review.

There are penalties, however, in the verse of a Donne. The 'conceits' are so self-conscious, so worked out for their own sake often enough, that we feel as much the nudge of the author's cleverness at our elbow as have our eyes on the subjects in question—with that wonderful transparency (for example) and perspicuousness of style which, I was insisting in my last chapter, characterizes the prose of *Agnes Grey*.

> Death be not proude, though some have called thee
> Mighty and dreadfull, for, thou art not soe,
> For, those, whom thou think'st, thou dost overthrow,
> Die not, poor death, nor yet canst thou kill mee.
> From rest and sleepe, which but thy pictures bee,
> Much pleasure, then from thee, much more must flow,
> And soonest our best men with thee doe goe,
> Rest of their bones, and soules deliverie.
> Thou art slave to Fate, Chance, kings, and desperate men,
> And dost with poyson, warre, and sicknesse dwell,
> And poppie, or charmes can make us sleepe as well,
> And better than thy stroake; why swell'st thou then?
> One short sleepe past, wee wake eternally,
> And death shall be no more; death, thou shalt die.

Is there any saw more recurrent or more fatuous in poetry than the comparison of death with sleep? Has no man alive ever beheld the two and remarked their infinitude of difference? As soon as the Duke in *Measure for Measure* (III, sc. i, lines 17–19) prepares Claudio for the terminal condition with that sort of apostrophe (himself of course a man due to carry on living), I know that, whatever Shakespeare consciously deliberated, he is the villain of the piece.

In sleep we recreate our bodies and minds; much of our most significant living is done through dreams, conscious and other; and anybody who has watched a sleeping human form will have looked, more often than not, upon beauty being vital; *Natura naturans*. Death is the cancellation of these things; if it were no less innocuous than sleep, why did God Himself weep inconsolably at his friends' (he could not bear it indeed, and called Lazarus back), why did He sweat in agony at the prospect of His own? We may well believe that by that very demise Death died and has been made a portal into felicity. I do. But the absolute bankruptcy of the equation, in logic and feeling— Death is only an extended kind of somnolence—leaps from every page which attempts the lie; and in this instance testifies to the very real limits beyond which a Metaphysical Muse ought not to transgress.

Others of the Holy Sonnets—for instance, 'Salvation to all

that will is nigh' or 'Batter my heart'—are deeply moving and powerful because there tough thinking penetrates and illuminates religious mysteries to bring them fresh upon our sense; cerebration extends the heart's kingdom. But here Donne is so concerned bravely to work up conceits against Death—the poem huffs and puffs—he has lost sight of the reality with which he is trying intellectually to juggle. A proof of the poem's failure is that by the end Mortality comes tramping back over the scene terrible as an army with banners. The author confesses as much in defying it with itself and acknowledging that the worst thing that can happen to any entity is to die. His very last phrase gives his whole game away; and the bravado generally rings hollow— draws itself up boldly only to collapse as a pinch of dust before the actuality of the Foe—not least because so much bravado of itself inevitably bespeaks dread. (Compare Herbert's far more relaxed and genuinely comforted handling of the theme.[1])

Of that sort of cleverness tripping itself up, intellect overreaching with 'conceits' (in both senses of the word) and wiredrawn paradox, we are wholly spared in Anne Brontë's verse. Charlotte's comment about her sister's poems having 'a sweet sincere pathos of their own' is apt in that sincerity, authenticity of feeling, is absolutely their keynote. A few of the early Gondal verses exhibit bits of the stock-in-trade of forced Romantic emotion, all but inevitably. Almost no poet starts off wholly underivative, and we feel in presence of truth, but truth on stilts, when Anne writes, in 'A Voice from the Dungeon' (No. 3), 'I uttered one long piercing shriek' or such a phrase as 'That cursed scream'. But in the main what we benefit from is a simplicity of diction which answers to neither more nor less nor other than a real apprehension. Compare with 'Death be not proud' the following (No. 31, pp. 100–1 of Chitham):

> Yes, thou art gone and never more
> Thy sunny smile shall gladden me;
> But I may pass the old church door
> And pace the floor that covers thee;
>
> May stand upon the cold damp stone
> And think that frozen lies below
> The lightest heart that I have known,
> The kindest I shall ever know.

Yet though I cannot see thee more
'Tis still a comfort to have seen,
And though thy transient life is o'er
'Tis sweet to think that thou hast been;

To think a soul so near divine
Within a form so angel fair
United to a heart like thine
Has gladdened once our humble sphere.

This may or may not refer to the Rev. Willy Weightman, Mr. Brontë's blithe flirtatious curate and it may, as the author may have done throughout her acquaintance with and remembrance of him, idealize its object. But the verses do not fake any part of the feelings as such that the beloved here has inspired; and though 'humble sphere' is a *bit* unctuous (yet even that is considerably justified by the references 'soul so near divine', 'form so angel fair'), the poem does not seek to step outside the limits of the truly felt and believed. The author averts her gaze from the Beyond for realization of an emotional interest which has here evidently been awakened but not fulfilled. That would be not only heretical—Anne Brontë like all other Christians has to believe there is no marrying or giving in marriage in Heaven—it would be meretricious wishfulness, an imposition upon the dead as upon reality. The whole is all the more poignant and moving *because* it does not stitch in after-life compensations for its speaker, though the speaker evidently believes in higher modes of being than the human-mortal. The poem registers loss and gratitude; and we feel the loss the more because those things come, in such a case, in that order.

We also fully appreciate the warmth, the gladness. The thematic point is made the more forcefully that, in a world where such visitations as *that* can have occurred, when we are confronted if only once in a lifetime with moral and physical beauty so apprehended, there is more to living than 'pacing the floor that covers thee' and to dying than a light heart lying frozen beneath a cold damp stone.

It is a brief work for one compacting so full a complex of feelings so finely balanced.

More impressive still perhaps is 'To Cowper' (No. 19, pp. 84–6).

Sweet are thy strains, Celestial Bard,
    And oft in childhood's years
I've read them o'er and o'er again
    With floods of silent tears.

The language of my inmost heart
    I traced in every line—
My sins, *my* sorrows, hopes and fears
    Were there, and only mine.

All for myself the sigh would swell,
    The tear of anguish start;
I little knew what wilder woe
    Had filled the poet's heart.

I did not know the nights of gloom,
    The days of misery,
The long long years of dark despair
    That crushed and tortured thee.

But they are gone, and now from earth
    Thy gentle soul is passed.
And in the bosom of its God
    Has found its Home at last.

It must be so if God is love
    And answers fervent prayer;
Then surely thou shalt dwell on high,
    And I may meet thee there.

Is He the source of every good,
    The spring of purity?
Then in thine hours of deepest woe
    Thy God was still with thee.

How else when every hope was fled
    Couldst thou so fondly cling
To holy things and holy men
    And how so sweetly sing—

Of things that God alone could teach?
    And whence that purity;
That hatred of all sinful ways,
    That gentle charity?

Are these the symptoms of a heart
 Of Heavenly grace bereft,
For ever banished from its God,
 To Satan's fury left?

Yet should thy darkest fears be true,
 If Heaven be so severe
That such a soul as thine is lost,
 O! how shall I appear?

One awkwardness had better be dispensed with and cleared
out of the way to begin with. I have to confess the first stanza
of this poem strikes me as unintentionally funny. It is too
schoolgirlish-hyperbolical, the 'floods of silent tears'. But that
pons asinorum once crossed, we are onto very firm ground
indeed; and there is nothing windily rhetorical, nothing use-
lessly exaggerated, in 'Celestial' of line 1. The whole poem
articulates about the problem—How are we to reconcile the
beliefs, both, that there are *animae naturaliter Christianae* in the
world—loving gentle spirits whose hearts yearn towards
God—and (as the words haunting Nancy Brown in *Agnes Grey*
affirm) 'Many shall seek to enter in, and shall not be able'? The
power of this series of lyrics is of course most visible in their
shocking ending, the surprise, for us readers, of concluding at
such a bleak terrible place after so much quiet honeyed dis-
tillation of sweetness and light. Artfully the author, as equally
theologian and rhapsode together, has led us up the very garden
path which precipitates upon the cliff-drop of Calvinist theory:
predestination and the momentous unworthiness even of 'good'
Believers. In so doing Anne Brontë crystallizes perfectly the
predicament haunting eighteenth- and nineteenth-century
Evangelical consciences: such as, for instance, not only
Cowper's but also Samuel Johnson's.

   It would be madness for me to set up in wisdom against the
Great Lexicographer and scarcely less dotty to attempt here a
full-blown theological treatise. I may walk here in matters
much out of my depth, as if (all unintentionally) mocking the
integuments of those great people's afflictions. Yet perhaps
even the least of us has corrective insights to afford one another
and add to the common world fund; and it seems to me that the
error their minds made was not caring too much about sanctity

and damnation (how can anybody care enough?), but doing so from the wrong end of the problem. When the best of the Saints have declared of all their own righteousness that it is 'filthy rags', and St. Thomas Aquinas, looking upon his theology said 'it reminded him of straw', to expect that prior to death one will have attained the infinite purity of being,

> A condition of complete simplicity
> (Costing not less than everything)[2]

which can inhabit and breathe inside the domain of the Mercy-Seat's acceptation, would be sanguine; though it means catastrophe not to be aiming at that each and every day, utterly. But the Gospels show Jesus's constant emphasis upon the 'heart'—in the sense of the central will—of an individual: what he or she turns their essential volition towards, of and in living; 'For where your heart is, there will be your treasure also.'

I deduce from this that Cowper's, Dr. Johnson's and, in her earlier life, Anne Brontë's, religious melancholy was a 'mistake'(!) in the sense that it arose from continually comparing their frailties within and the perfection of the standard required, of desires and conduct. This is not the whole point: 'For in Thy sight shall no man living be justified.' The key issue, I infer, is whether the individual has really striven to walk in the narrow way and through the strait gate.

Of course that can be seen as just putting the predicament back by a step or two of logic. How can we know, of something so deceitful as our hearts, whether we really *are* enrolled among those who hunger and thirst after righteousness?

One answer is (as was illustrated in the last chapter) to walk fervently in the law of the Lord. We become, as creatures of habit, what we pretend to be.

Another is that our knowledge of ourselves, at this outset of our existence, presumably is not expected—it cannot be—as competent as our guardian angels' (and the Devil's), though self-examination of a regular healthy kind is obligatory.

A third is that 'all things are possible to the mercy of God', including

> the purification of the motive
> In the ground of our beseeching.[3]

Finally, *an element* of dread is probably a wholesome thing and ought to haunt the purlieus of our religious feeling, because in the last analysis complacency means ruin and judgement is not going to rest with us. As Philip Larkin has said, but in connection with Old Age, of which it seems to me less true,

> Can they never tell
> What is dragging them back, and how it will end? Not at night?
> Not when the strangers come? Never, throughout
> The whole hideous inverted childhood? Well,
> We shall find out.[4]

Talk is cheap of course, and all this is extremely easy to write. For the vastly more important task of living these commitments through in their individual cases I am little qualified to have advised the figures of our literary history here named. All I would yet add is that an obsession with one's possible damnation does seem as non-religious in essential motivation— because un-God-centred—as the bland smug confidence of a self-righteous Pharisee.

Thus a characteristic theological blindspot of two centuries back. (In our day—we needn't boast—is not their name Legion, and most of them buzzingly gaining an upper hand in the Synod of the English Church with its horrible liturgical 'reform' [= mutilation] and most questionable doctrinal changes?)

It is a blindspot (if I have understood the matter aright), but also a perpetual human concern. 'To Cowper' is not a poem we can look over as with the sense of just turning leaves in an archive. How can God be loving, and some of His creatures— and yet they be damned? How can we come to terms with ourselves, transfixed between the wish to be good and the knowledge of the slimy things that are given house-room and nourished in our hearts? We look for symptoms of virtue in ourselves and even may find some (ll. 29–36). Yet we know, or know of, others far advanced in moral calibre beyond our own personalities and accomplishments who all but despair of their characters and behaviour.

To come to terms with this dilemma appears to have been a

major—perhaps the major—task in Anne Brontë's life; and the force of this poem signifies the difficulty of the gulf she had laboriously to traverse in pain of mind, body and spirit before she arrived at peace.

Part of the work's strength is its very conventionality of language. Her editor notes that from a study of her manuscripts

> the initial impression is that revision is often in the direction of simplicity or accuracy. Words felt to be too rhetorical seem to be suppressed in favour of simpler vocabulary—though such vocabulary usually remains within the hymn or ballad convention; there is no attempt to assimilate to everyday language.
>
> Rhyme is often starkly economical. There appears to be a deliberate attempt to reduce or restrict the number of line endings. For example in No. 55 the lines in stanza nine end *thrill/appal, still/all*, the four closing consonants being the same. Two verses later all the vowels are the same: *thine/eyes, mine/prize*. This example could be paralleled many times over. It seems likely that the intention is to pare down to essentials, in the same way as rhetoric is suppressed and anti-romantic views are preferred to flamboyant ones.[5]

We need to add to this quite specifically that the rhymes, like the metrics, practically never surprise; but this is not only a limitation, it also tells for a strength. We know that 'years' will be matched with 'tears' in stanza 1 of 'To Cowper'; 'line' and 'mine' in stanza 2; that 'at last' will marry 'is passed' in 4, etc. As with George Crabbe we can nearly always anticipate what the line-endings are going to be; likewise that very few of them will be interestingly 'run-on'. There is in both authors' verses none of the continuous surprisingness which characterizes Alexander Pope:

> This nymph, to the destruction of mankind,
> Nourish'd two Locks, which graceful hung behind
> In equal curls, and well conspir'd to deck
> With shining ringlets the smooth iv'ry neck.
> Love in these labyrinths his slaves detains,
> And mighty hearts are held in slender chains.
> With hairy sprindges we the birds betray,
> Slight lines of hair surprize the finny prey,
> Fair tresses man's imperial race insnare,
> And beauty draws us with a single hair.

('Rape of the Lock')

And for this very reason they are not placed among our Great Poets. But their conventionality of expression has itself a virtue. As moralists with ancient themes, their expectable methods, and rhymes used in traditional combinations, remind us how many have trod the same way before, what immemorial truths they are telling. The unsurprisingness of the diction—with import and skill enough nevertheless in the matter and its management to make their poems (for the most part) interesting and significant—works like the mnemonics in Homeric poetry. Just as we feel 'Ah yes, all the time there in the background, reliably going on, *being*, is the wine-purple sea (or) flashing-eyed Athena', so with Anne Brontë as with Crabbe we say to ourselves, 'Yes, these are the habitual sensations of the religiously struggling, the morally all but overpowered. I am not alone in my difficulties and my reliefs. Others have been here before me. It is a road with recognizable contours.'

The Brontë Sisters' writings are full of unhappiness, defeat, frustration. These express themselves in works alternately embodying feelings of imprisonment, heroic outlawry, and despair: the captive in her cage is subject to varying moods and by turns beats on the bars, slumps in despondency and is exhilarated by visions of freedom. A more substantial release they find in Nature, and one element of power in Anne's traditionalist verse is her response to the natural environment. It is as freshly felt, if not as freshly expressed, as the great Romantic poets'.

'The Bluebell' for instance is an elegiac poem recording lost childhood and happiness, but the bloom which provokes this meditation is registered not only as a matrix of poignant recollection, a trigger of Proustian reminiscence: it is seen in its own character, and this brings the lyric's whole process to life.

> Whence came that rising in my throat,
> That dimness in my eye?
> Why did those burning drops distil—
> Those bitter feelings rise?

> O, that lone flower recalled to me
> My happy childhood's hours
> *When bluebells seemed like fairy gifts*
> *A prize among the flowers*, . . .
>
> (ll. 29–36, p. 74, emphasis added)

Similarly it is the actualizing of her domestic landscape in 'Home' (pp. 99–100) which makes the loneliness and longing that are that poem's principal subject so vivid to us:

> But give me back my barren hills
>   Where colder breezes rise:
>
> Where scarce the scattered, stunted trees
>   Can yield an answering swell,
> But where a wilderness of heath
>   Returns the sound as well. . . .
>
> Restore to me that little spot,
>   With gray walls compassed round,
> Where knotted grass neglected lies,
>   And weeds usurp the ground.

'Knotted grass' and still more 'weeds *usurp*' there make the work rise practically to greatness. (Indeed is it not a feature of great poetry, as such—this a friend, himself a poet, once remarked to me—that it has 'strong' verbs? *Their* imaginativeness was, in his view, both origin and touchstone of a given talent's power.) *Thus*, we feel, the great sisters of Haworth Parsonage saw their immediate environment: with truth and affection, romance and realism equally keen.

Love figures prominently in Anne Brontë's work but not as a fiery intermingling of souls and a method of release from mere corporeal life, as with Emily; nor as escape from woman's servitude and boredom as in Charlotte's pages. The Four Loves—Agape, Philadelphia, Caritas and Eros—are almost fused in one sentiment with the youngest Brontë, and this her poems feelingly illustrate.

One of her first surviving verses expresses the dream of young love and its fulfilment—though temporarily barred by separation and exile: 'Alexander and Zenobia' (No. 2 in Chitham's edition). But in the main her earliest work utters

strong feelings of imprisonment and loss; and these are not less
significant for being Gondal poems. Economy and, with it, yet
more intensity of misery comes with her twenty-first year of
life. The 'Lines written at Thorp Green' and dated 25 August
1840 (No. 11 of Chitham) approach to realizing Tennyson's
power in 'Mariana at the moated grange':

> O! I am very weary
>   Though tears no longer flow;
> My eyes are tired of weeping,
>   My heart is sick of woe.
>
> My life is very lonely,
>   My days pass heavily;
> I'm weary of repining,
>   Wilt thou not come to me?
>
> Oh didst thou know my longings
>   For thee from day to day,
> My hopes so often blighted,
>   Thou wouldst not thus delay.

The new master touch there is the numbness implicit in 'tears'
(line 2) not being possessively qualified: it is as if the speaker
looks on her own emotions now with detachment induced by
extreme suffering. But the force of frustrated love in this author
directs itself outward to sympathy at large with mankind.

This is expressed, self-abnegatively as it were, in No. 39
where the poet begs to be released from life if God will send
'No freshening dew'—

> If friendship's solace must decay
>   When other joys are gone;
> And love must keep so far away
>   While I go wandering on:

and finds its most aggrieved utterance in 'A Word to the
Calvinists', repudiating the doctrine of predestination and
embracing that of universalism;

> And O! there lives within my heart
> A hope long nursed by me, . . .
>
> That as in Adam all have died
> In Christ shall all men live . . .

That even the wicked shall at last
Be fitted for the skies
And when their dreadful doom is past
To light and life arise

is how its positive faith concludes, having demanded of 'the
Elect'

But is it sweet to look around and view
Thousands excluded from that happiness,
Which they deserve at least as much as you,
Their faults not greater nor their virtues less?

'The Captive Dove' elucidates these elements combining in
Anne Brontë's thought. The free spirit longs to roam freely, in
a natural environment which is warm and happy. By implication the proximity of a mate, 'one faithful dear companion',
would be compensation for its loss of liberty because one
element in such fulfilments, not the whole. It is almost as if
human love's use is seen as a consolation to the Soul in its exile
from Heaven. Yet it is also a part of Heaven.

The last stanza of 'Weep not too much, my darling' shows
Nature, amorous Love, and Incarceration in an alien fate, all
fused as experiences which can be made to fructify from each
other:

O, scorn not Nature's bounties!
   My soul partakes with thee.
Drink bliss from all her fountains,
   Drink for thyself and me!
Say not, 'My soul is buried
   In dungeon gloom with thine;'
But say, '*His* heart is here with me;
   His spirit drinks with mine.'

The fruit of their inter-animation and its development in
Anne Brontë's thought is ripest in one of her last poems
(No. 55 of Chitham): 'Severed and gone, so many years!'
which bears the date April 1847. All sorts of ability now
inhabit her pen. For instance, one verse concludes 'That thou
art gone so far away.' The next begins 'For ever gone'; and in
its context it has almost as fine an effect as the echoing of
'Forlorn!' in Keats's 'Ode to a Nightingale'.

This is another meditation, now that further time has elapsed, on the Beloved who has been lost in death. Lengthier than 'Night' (No. 37 'Written early in 1845') or 'Yes thou art gone', it is also more substantial in achieving complex sensations of great beauty.

It starts by repudiating the idea of the Beloved's identity as 'festering there in slow decay' where

> The charnel moisture never dries
> From the dark flagstones o'er its breast, (ll. 11–12)

and reveals that superstitious yearning which is often one of the afflictions of bereavement:

> I, by night,
> Have prayed, within my silent room,
> That Heaven would grant a burst of light
> Its cheerless darkness to illume;
>
> And give thee to my longing eyes,
> A moment, as thou shinest now,
> Fresh from thy mansion in the skies,
> With all its glories on thy brow.

In her longing the poet is willing even to brave what might well be the terrors of such an apparition:

> A shape these human nerves would thrill,
> A majesty that might appal,

in confidence of the other's good nature and transfigured humanity—

> Did not thy earthly likeness, still,
> Gleam softly, gladly, through it all.

This 'False hope! vain prayer!' has not been granted, though the author confesses to having actually 'called on Heaven . . .—called on thee' for a manifestation.

Then she realizes how little in fact she does possess of the lost object of her devotion; not even a lock of hair remains to her (41–4); and the concluding movement of the poem into affirmation is all the more effective because the psychological honesty which has been its hallmark all through is maintained. Wonderfully fluent, newly *easy*, in feeling and verse, has Anne

Brontë's art now become. Exquisite the 'chill' of line 51, for example, working as does great poetry for a variety of effects— not least with the slight hiatus of breath necessitated by its place at the line's ending—mutually and harmoniously com- pacting a matrix of important meanings. Best of all the psychological fidelity and spiritual truth realized in what follows:

> Thou breathest in my bosom yet,
> And dwellest in my beating heart;
> And, while I cannot quite forget,
> Thou, darling, canst not quite depart. (ll. 53–6)

Those lines confess that indeed, in fact, she will partly forget, will cumulatively idealize and alter him—and has done so from the moment of their last separation. It is like the operative work of the word 'smokeless' in Wordsworth's 'Westminster Bridge' sonnet where the bard beholds the city's features 'All bright and glittering in the smokeless air'—which conveys not only the clarity of the early morning London atmosphere but also intimates that the capital is a coal-burning aggregation which will awake later to industrial activity, throwing off its dawn-tide rural garb.

Yet there is no loss or disparagement in this admission. 'And, while I cannot quite forget' implies not only that she will do so somewhat, owing to the sheer activity of Time; also that she does not want to *nor will ever entirely do so* or falsify the dead Beloved in her memory of him. The relaxedness of the rhythm hereabout, especially at 'Thou, darling, canst', testifies to his influence in the world and upon her as benefic *now*; and what is most moving of all is for us to intuit, from the very process of the work, how this influence has brought her from attention to bereavement, frustration, misery and (really therefore) *self* to outward-looking, grateful, creative consciousness. The poem witnesses irrefrageably of itself to the truth it promulgates:

> Life seems more sweet that thou didst live,
> And men more true that thou wert one. . . . (ll. 61–2)

To this affirmation the very last phrase of all testifies yet more. Its author confesses sharing her devotion to the dead man and, in a beautiful way, that the experience of him has

nourished more lives than one, her own, enamoured of him.
That she can generously thus acknowledge his role in other
existences tells how much a cogency for emotional giving,
moral warmth and happiness he has of himself exerted—or
she has made of him: it comes to the same thing.

> Earth has received thine earthly part;
> Thine heavenly flame has heavenward flown;
> But both still linger in my heart,
> Still live, and not in mine alone.

Perhaps the most valuable way of reading Anne Brontë's
verse, however, is as a single work—which is all the more
feasible in that it is no large, let alone over-extended corpus.
For it has an important unity, from the way it addresses itself
as one mind continually wrestling with the problem explicit in
one of its very titles, 'Fluctuations'. This author regularly uses
personae indeed, but we don't differentiate her, in feeling, from
them as much as we do Robert Browning from Bishop
Bloughram or the Duke of Ferrara (of 'My Last Duchess') in
his dramatic monologues. The 'Verses by Lady Geralda' which
open the chronological sequence that, in as far as it can be
accurately established, I am recommending as appropriate for
study in the nature of one *opus*, are written by an historical
person actually 16 years old. But its nostalgic references to
'long ago' when the speaker

> loved to lie
> Upon the pathless moor

are not incompatible with adolescent 'sentiments to which
every bosom returns an echo'.

The grieving mother 'Marina Sabia' of 'A Voice from the
Dungeon' (No. 3), the narrator of 'The Parting' (No. 6), the
warrior who utters 'Z——'s Dream' (No. 53) et cetera: these
are not Anne Brontë and yet they are. For even the imagination
of heroic outlawry—and *its* spiritual disablements—are one of
her ways of registering the life of frustration which her poems
alone plainly adumbrate. She felt as keenly as Charlotte, it is
clear, her existence of social, intellectual, emotional and

professional inanition. Those sisters experienced in a rare
degree of torture the diagnosis I quoted before: 'We are constructed for full living. Occasion rarely offers.' Highly intelligent and educated, intensely creative and feeling, their geo-
graphic, social and financial circumstances were such as to
combine maximum aspiration with minimum fulfilment. The
gap between what the Brontë children were brought up to
hope of life—not least by their own native degree of mental
activity and emotional richness—and what it could actually
offer them, was all but crippling. It crippled Branwell.

What starts off as slightly factitious hyperbole, a Byronic
rhetoric of loss, loneliness, imprisonment and defeat becomes
most poignantly the hard facts of the adult case, as we read
these poems in sequence. Yet their author does not stay fixated
there, to wallow in self-pity, projected onto melodramatic
situations and outcast figures: nor in lyrics of mere absolute
lament. Her condition is much too painful for any such indulgence and she has far too fine a spirit. Successively her themes
of frustration (in several kinds), bereavement, religious
feeling—not least the coming to terms with Calvinist doctrine
(imprinted by her aunt)—and Nature as energizing relief, are
more deeply apprehended and fused as she works towards a
very hard-won Christian response to this whole predicament.

Part of the difficulty of so doing is expressed in No. 33: we
do not achieve a high tableland of equable consciousness, after
whatever belaboured difficulty, and then stay there.

> And darker, drearier fell the night
>   Upon my spirit then;
> But what is that faint struggling light—
>   Is it the moon again?
>
> Kind Heaven, increase that silvery gleam
>   And bid these clouds depart;
> And let her kind and holy beam
>   Restore my fainting heart.

The coming and going of the 'Moon's' gleam—i.e. reflected
light—within the spirit is itself to be traced in the verse-series
that her work as a whole affords.

This is what makes it a spiritual autobiography of no mean

import and gives so much force and conviction to her renewed and ever renewed attempts to reconcile feeling with the discipline of reason.

The dialogue between Hope and Experience which is No. 42 (published in the 1846 volume as 'Views of Life') expressed, as does more maturely 'Self-Communion' (No. 57), the central crux: how to live with all these human affections in a sphere of disappointment and (therein) how to cope with Time. It incorporates the otherwise slightly juvenile quality of the 'late' Gondal poems (e.g. Nos. 50–3)—in that they regress to the appetite for heroic situations and glamorous outlawry, a world of free yet fraught enterprise—and what is the overplus of a sense of unhappiness in the collected poems as a whole. Coming to terms with those things was what Anne Brontë's life, as recorded in her poetic *oeuvre*, was about.

By the end (Nos. 55–9) this is what she has magnificently achieved. In this later work there is more control of materials which are more complex, than previously; for example, 'Self-Communion', though uncharacteristically long (334 lines), is not a sprawl but a retrospect at once freely moving and, with intrinsic logic, of progressive discovery: one proof of which is the fact that the author varies her metric and thus avoids monotony, without our feeling that the rhythmical changes are contrived or other than a function of the quietly meditative voice moving at its own appropriate variety of pace.

Reconciliation of the self to Life's disappointments: that is the poem's theme, nowhere more poignantly embodied than in Anne's account of her relationship with (almost certainly and inevitably) her sister Emily.

> Oh, I have known a wondrous joy
> In early friendship's pure delight,—
> A genial bliss that could not cloy—
> My sun by day, my moon by night.
> Absence, indeed, was sore distress,
> And thought of death was anguish keen,
> And there was cruel bitterness
> When jarring discords rose between;
> And sometimes it was grief to know
> My fondness was but half returned.
> But this was nothing to the woe

> With which another truth was learned:—
> That I must check, or nurse apart
> Full many an impulse of the heart
>   And many a darling thought:
> What my soul worshipped, sought, and prized,
> Were slighted, questioned, or despised;—
>   this pained me more than aught.
> And as my love the warmer glowed
> The deeper would that anguish sink,
> That this dark stream between us flowed,
> Though both stood bending o'er its brink.

(Amazing, rich, profound, that metaphor!)

> Until, at last, I learned to bear
> A colder heart within my breast;
> To share such thoughts as I could share,
>   And calmly keep the rest.
> I saw that they were sundered now,
> The trees that at the root were one:
> They yet might mingle leaf and bough,
> But still the stems must stand alone. (ll. 178–207)

This is a type of our earthly condition really: the things we most set our hearts on and live by; well, they prove transient or essentially flawed in the end, the objects of misprision or the victims of change. It is of a piece with the total process of her poetic output, however—by turns exhilarated, painfilled, downcast and blithe—that by now Anne Brontë securely identifies this frustration, like her others, as a pointer to the only true happiness at the sole Abiding City:

> So must it fare with all thy race
> Who seek in earthly things their joy:
> So fading hopes lost hopes shall chase, . . . (ll. 261–63)

It is not a refusal of earthly loves which is in question: no frigidity of feeling is come, reacting to rejection by them. On the contrary, much of the work is a long warm paean on their felicity, their nutrient value:

> O vainly might I seek to show
> The joys from happy love that flow!
> The warmest words are all too cold
> The secret transports to unfold

70

Of simplest word or softest sigh,
Or from the glancing of an eye
   To say what rapture beams;
One look that bids our fears depart,
And well assures the trusting heart
It beats not in the world alone—
Such speechless raptures I have known,
   But only in my dreams. (ll. 233–44)

The admission at the close of that verse-paragraph does more than all to substantiate the whole suffrage Anne Brontë offers mortal mutualities. But what comes to us, with the full authority of experience and personally avouched awareness, are the 'home truths', as one may name them, of the conclusion:

Toil is my glory—Grief my gain,
If God's approval they obtain.

So much has been won that when she next writes, it is a hymn of great authority that in a sense sums up the argument achieved by its predecessors. There are 'realms of joy':

But he who seeks that blest abode
Must all his powers employ.
   (No. 58, 'Believe not those who say', ll. 6–8)

And what is so fine is that, like George Herbert, Anne is now in a condition to apprehend old verities in a new way. Moving indeed the freshness of feeling at

And there amid the sternest heights,
The sweetest flowerets gleam;—

or

On all her breezes borne
Earth yields no scents like those; . . . (ll. 11–14)

By the end she has become a poet capable of things quietly extraordinary; and—though much of her earlier work functions with great felicity of expression and has an absolute value— getting progressively better.

NOTES

1. In his poem 'Death', *The Works of George Herbert*, ed. F. E. Hutchinson (Oxford, 1945), p. 185.
2. T. S. Eliot, *Four Quartets*, 'Little Gidding' (V, 40–1).
3. Ibid., conclusion of section III.
4. *High Windows* (cit. supra), p. 20.
5. Edward Chitham, *The Poems of Anne Brontë: A New Text and Commentary* (London, 1979), p. 32.

3

The Tenant of Wildfell Hall:
Reality's Anarchism

If *The Tenant of Wildfell Hall* is a failure—and I think that, on two counts, it has to be so denominated—it is a great failure: one which leaves all sorts of literary achievements we call successes well behind. The flaws are (1) the author's handling of erotic motivations and (2) the overall control of her material, of which, on our part, we sense she does not securely reign in possession. We do not feel, closing the book, as with *Wuthering Heights* that the whole thing has been accomplished by the writer's creative intention, answering to itself. Yet that caveat is present with us just exactly because, by the time we do turn its final page, we have been through a very big experience indeed and one that, deliberately challenging Emily Brontë's novel as in some sort it is, by no means comes out of the combat crestfallen or with the palms all awarded on one side.

It is like Jane Austen's *Sense and Sensibility* in working, at a primary level, as a moralist's cautionary tale—a warning to the gullible or the emotionally uneducated—and one which is well realized. But additionally it throws, like Austen's first publication, so much more into the measure than that formula (careful-parable-about-living) bargains for.

The novel presents itself in the form of a story within a story. Gilbert Markham, a gentleman farmer, is setting forth the unusual history of his courtship and marriage in younger days, for his brother-in-law (the husband of his sister Rose) Halford. A necessarily lengthy narrative of the early stages in his wooing of Helen Graham, the 'Tenant' of the whole book's

title, gives way, about a quarter of the work through, to Mrs.
'Graham's' own account of her previous and unhappy matrimony. She is a figure of mystery to the Northern rural neigh-
bourhood in which the tale opens and where she has come in
search of seclusion with her very young son Arthur during 'the
autumn of 1827'.

For her earnest life of a recluse and her fierce views on
temperance the community at first mocks, then comes to
suspect her. Finally they persecute her on the supposition that
she has a vicious past and no amended ways. Not the least
part of this punishment is inflicted by Markham himself who,
having fallen in love with this elegant beautiful unorthodox
woman (she is also a fine painter and appears to get her living
by her art), pesters her with his devotion and quite seriously
wounds Mr. Lawrence the local squire and landlord of the
Hall, when he suspects him of being a favoured rival and
bringing its fair lady's name into disrepute. Anger turns to
chill misery however when, eavesdropping, he hears both Mr.
Lawrence and Mrs. Graham—now the object of moral oppro-
brium even upon the parish vicar's lips—talking to one another
on the forecourt of the delapidated but partially restored
property that is her present refuge, as if indeed possessed of a
secret and illicit understanding.

Markham swallows his pride enough, all the same, eventually to benefit from an *éclaircissement*. Her story is quite different from what he has assumed and, chronologically set forth as
it is in her Diary, she cuts painful long explanation short in the
medium of a personal interview by giving it to him to read.

Here begins Chapter 16 of the book (and it continues her
narrative till near the very close of Chapter 44) with an
account that takes us further back again: to 1821, when Helen
has met and mutually engaged attentions with Arthur
Huntingdon, a debonair handsome society man, whom her
aunt advises her against as having the reputation of loose
living and rake-helly companions. Young as she is (18), she
gains her distant father's consent and that of the uncle-guardian
under whose roof she dwells; Huntingdon weds her and her
considerable patrimony; and Helen sets out on her self-
appointed task of reforming the blemishes out of her gay if
worldly husband's character: for she adores him and has all

along cherished the expectation of functioning in his life like a guardian angel.

At first things go reasonably well. Though some of his conversation during their courtship has boded ill enough, life at their Grassdale Manor out in the country is one of rural pursuits and contentments. But by 25 March of the next year—after three months of wedded solitude—Huntingdon, who has no profession, trade or other occupation, is bored with this routine and adjourns back to London, at first accompanied by his wife, then staying there alone.

Now begins anew the cycle of dissipation and reform which is evidently a part of his past and in which the whole of the rest of his future is worn away. When not enjoying visits of several months' duration, and very heavy drinking, in the capital, he brings coarse company to the Manor and gets the liquor and foul jests to flow liberally there. Eventually it transpires he is conducting an adulterous liaison with Annabella Wilmot, a beautiful but heartless woman now married to his erewhile gaming and swilling companion Lord Lowborough. She is the spoiled predator in *that* marriage and the whole situation is all the more poignant in that Lowborough's devotion to his wife is clearly the lynch-pin of his happiness (almost his sanity) in this world; as it has likewise been of his reformation, originally, from an alcoholic gambler into a character of courageous integrity. Discovery of his wife's unfaithfulness almost provokes the peer (whose fortitude against his own inclinations to the intemperance of the past has alone truly earned him the epithet 'noble') to suicide. In his hostess Helen Huntingdon's case however, despair has long since wrought practically its worst: she has all but lost hope of her spouse's character and is now principally concerned with his influence upon her sole child's. The property and marriage-laws of her time are such that everything becomes an aggravation of misery:

> I am a slave—a prisoner—but that is nothing; if it were myself alone I would not complain, but I am forbidden to rescue my son from ruin, and what was once my only consolation is become the crowning source of my despair. . . .

She has become a prisoner indeed by the date (Ch. 40) that is written in the journal to which she nightly confides and by means of which she can reason with herself. For Huntingdon, having caught her penning it and discovered there her plan to make a getaway with her son, has all but stripped her of the means of escape: her jewels (with which she hoped to pay for an establishment of her own far off) and her paintings (laboriously executed and collected over the long months to provision the future in some such hiding-place). Yet she has the countenance of both her old nurse Rachel and the butler at Grassdale, no less daunted than she by the grossnesses of the house; and, throwing herself upon her brother's assistance, flees one very early morning in the October of little Arthur's fourth year, with that offspring and her ancient servant.

The fraternal relative who has prepared a refuge for her is none other than the Mr. Lawrence Gilbert Markham has so much misunderstood; and indeed amity between these two in the remainder of what follows never becomes very brilliant, though Markham goes, after reading all this, to offer a sincere apology for the grievous boorishness and blood-violence of which he has been guilty upon the person of the rescuer of Helen Huntingdon (*née* Lawrence).

Her husband is beginning now to be really stricken in health by his indulgences. He also fails to prise from any source the secret of her whereabouts, but the report of his own collapse sends her, feeling duty-bound, back to nurse him; though she withholds their son till he has signed an agreement making the boy over to her governance. The occasion proves his last chance of physical rescue. She writes to her brother:

> He is decidedly better, but very low from the depressing effects of his severe illness and the strict regimen he is obliged to observe—so opposite to all his previous habits. It is deplorable to see how completely his past life has degenerated his once noble constitution, and vitiated the whole system of his organization. But the doctor says he may now be considered out of danger, if he will only continue to observe the necessary restrictions. Some stimulating cordials he must have, but they should be judiciously diluted and sparingly used; and I find it very difficult to keep him to this. At first, his extreme dread of death rendered the task an easy one; but in proportion as he feels his acute suffering abating, and sees the danger receding, the more intractable he becomes.

Fatally he gives rein to the alcoholic desire once more and Chapter 49 details, without morbidity but in grim realism, his dreadful death-agony:

> Oh, Frederick! [she writes] none can imagine the miseries, bodily and mental, of that death-bed! How could I endure to think that that poor trembling soul was hurried away to ever-lasting torment? it would drive me mad. But, thank God, I have hope—not only from a vague dependence on the possibility that penitence and pardon might have reached him at the last, but from the blessed confidence that, through whatever purging fires the erring spirit may be doomed to pass—whatever fate awaits it—still it is not lost, and God, who hateth nothing that He hath made, will bless it in the end!

Markham's joy at this release is undisguised (and at least it is not hypocritical); but his hopes receive several checks from the deliberate inadequacy of Lawrence as a go-between (Helen is now the heiress to two substantial estates and her brother does not like his frequent visitor sufficiently to have no fears for his sister's future married happiness) and from mis-understandings between the couple themselves, who have already suffered much from their declared mutual love and its frustration under the ban of her wretched wedlock. Paying a visit, however, from which he almost turns back unseen when he learns the extent of her new fortune, Gilbert is encouraged in his original hopes by the lady of the Hall at Staningley, where now she lives; and with the proviso that her aunt, its former mistress, can continue to dwell there till her demise, their matrimony the following August is agreed upon by all parties.

With an added brief retrospect over 'how happily my Helen and I have lived together, and how blessed we still are in each other's society, and in the promising young scions that are growing up about us', Markham concludes the whole.

Such a summary will have implied, if not the near-banal and anti-climactic simplicity of which I feared my plot-sketch from *Agnes Grey* was redolent before, then more grievously a kind of simple-minded ethics on the author's part which are far from engaging; as if a critic should be moved to complain: 'Yes. A dreadfully correct pious female marries a rake, he goes from bad to worse, dies; and she at last gets everything: two fortunes and a different worthier husband. Unless we are to set this down as an unworthy combination of vindictive moralizing and feminine wishfulness, so what?'

But that would be to judge solely from the outline I have offered. *The Tenant* in its reality is vastly more substantial and satisfying. For one thing Anne Brontë is well aware that it takes two to make an unsuccessful marriage. Not only has the heroine herself to thank for getting into this matrimonial trap, her awful match with Huntingdon, in the first place, against reasonable advice, good evidence and her own best judge-ment. Both she and the book attribute the blame where it is due—herself—through all that follows, and there is no question of our ever being allowed to develop sympathy for her as a woman who was wronged by a social conspiracy, or unmiti-gated ignorance, or any other moral alibi. Spiritual pride combined with inexperience got her into the mess; these things make her a being long tormented and leave her heavily scarred; and whether through her Preface to the second edition or in the whole tone and trajectory of the text itself, the author operates no double standard of blame for the male and excuse for the female parties to the tie. We pity Helen Huntingdon, very much; so does her creator. But the novel does not collude in any subtle process of exculpation for her original errors, however 'very natural'.

> I would not be understood to suppose that the proceedings of the unhappy scapegrace, with his few profligate companions I have here introduced, are a specimen of the common practices of society—the case is an extreme one, as I trusted none would fail to perceive; but I know that such characters do exist, and if I have warned one rash youth from following in their steps, or prevented one thoughtless girl from falling into the very natural error of my heroine, the book has not been written in vain.
>
> (Preface)

That tone is characteristic of the even-handedness with which the novelist here approaches and handles her personages throughout.

In this very spirit the book fairly canvasses also those 'active' faults in women which help their menfolk to defect. On the one hand, it can be a too great pliableness, as is exemplified in the interchange between Milicent (*née* Hargrave) and her spouse Hattersley, in Chapter 32, concerning his wandering heart.

> 'True, but adoration isn't love. I adore Annabella, but I don't love her; and I love thee, Milicent, but I don't adore thee.' In proof of his affection, he clutched a handful of her light brown ringlets, and appeared to twist them unmercifully.
>
> 'Do you really, Ralph?' murmured she, with a faint smile beaming through her tears, just putting up her hand to his, in token that he pulled rather too hard.
>
> 'To be sure I do,' responded he: 'only you bother me rather, sometimes.'
>
> 'I bother you!' cried she, in very natural surprise.
>
> 'Yes, you—but only by your exceeding goodness. When a boy has been eating raisins and sugar-plums all day, he longs for a squeeze of sour orange by way of a change. And did you never, Milly, observe the sands on the sea-shore; how nice and smooth they look, and how soft and easy they feel to the foot? But if you plod along, for half an hour, over this soft, easy carpet—giving way at every step, yielding the more the harder you press,—you'll find it rather wearisome work, and be glad enough to come to a bit of good, firm rock, that won't budge an inch whether you stand, walk, or stamp upon it; and, though it be hard as the nether millstone, you'll find it the easier footing after all.'

Though in the main the point is that Arthur Huntingdon will not learn, change, concede and compromise to make his marriage work, we do not entirely withhold understanding when he complains of his wife's cheerless rectitude, her disapproving starched presence. He is the villain of the piece in that, having started out with a lovely woman who adored him, he has by his behaviour gradually forced her devotion cold, turned it to stone, and got her altogether into a false position. If she endorses his licentiousness, of bottle and tongue, in the smallest degree, she perverts her own principles and poisons the future of her child; but what other role will she have chosen if she is a frolic element in his carousals?

He has left her only one option—to *be* the Spectre at the Feast—so we attribute most of the blame to him; but that that is evidently a self-defeating part in any attempt to purify such a household and union, Anne Brontë is evidently conscious.

> 'And what good did your gratitude do? I deluded myself with the idea that you were ashamed of your transgressions, and hoped you would never repeat them again; but now you have left me nothing to hope!'
> 'My case is quite desperate, is it? A very blessed consideration, if it will secure me from the pain and worry of my dear anxious wife's efforts to convert me, and her from the toil and trouble of such exertions, and her sweet face and silver accents from the ruinous effects of the same. A burst of passion is a fine rousing thing upon occasion, Helen, and a flood of tears is marvellously affecting, but, when indulged too often, they are both deuced plaguy things for spoiling one's beauty and tiring out one's friends.' (Ch. 30)

That is how the vicious circle of incompatibility begins to demonstrate itself, which his original dissipations have started up. Inevitably a glittering laughing merry coquette like Annabella Lowborough is going to appeal as antidote to a wife cast in the role there enforced, no less than flattering his roué's vanity and satisfying him erotically.

Yet we cannot complain, either, that Helen proves merely a moping plaintiff of a presence. That also would forfeit our sympathy and the validity of the book's debate. At the outset when she remonstrates with her husband she is feminine and beguiling (unconsciously) of manner: e.g.

> 'Arthur,' continued I, relaxing my hold of his arm, 'you don't love me half as much as I do you; and yet, if you loved me far less than you do, I would not complain, provided you loved your Maker more. I should rejoice to see you at any time so deeply absorbed in your devotions that you had not a single thought to spare for me. But, indeed, I should lose nothing by the change, for the more you loved your God the more deep and pure and true would be your love to me.' (Ch. 23)

This is not a choking indigestible gobbet of sanctimoniousness but a young girl's ardent enthusiasm for both loves, her religious creed and her spouse, which fuse in her artless idealism into very good theology (Danteanly expressed) and are offered from a rapturous heart all ingenuously. He has married a beauty who is not a bore; or rather, she becomes so only as he forces that function upon her.

Really the book is so faithful an accountant of human nature it works at a deep level as one of the most solidly embodied pieces of determinism ever sent forth into the world. Arthur Huntingdon and Helen Lawrence move, though with the sense of their own individuality and free choices, foredoomed along the rails of their identities to the differing termini thereon, and we have a sense of oversight and penetration into their affairs as full and as helpless as Wagner represents those of the seers of Valhalla. The gods can only tinker with men's destinies, not take away their intrinsic selfhoods, freedoms—and their dooms. Anne Brontë's psychology is not so other, though much less laboured, than Proust's, in seeing people's inextricability from their own natures and the consequences which follow.

Where she is kinder and fairer than Proust is in admitting the possibilities of amelioration in a particular instance. The prison-cells which are our current identities may not lack, in a given case, doors marked 'Exit, to freedom'; nor may a visitor (human or circumstantial) always be wanting, with the appropriate key. Lowborough and Hattersley have within their very characters the possibility of drastically improved living and under such influence as Helen's, instruction gained by pain-filled experience, they do in fact change for the better.

Like much else in this book it is artistry of a high order that weaves in the sub-plots of Lowborough's history and Hattersley's—in so unobtrusive and integrated a fashion. For their doings, in different ways (which contrast of itself has a value), suggest life's various chances and movements of change for the better. His lordship's earlier life is recapitulated by Huntingdon to Helen during their courtship—how he was a hard-drinking and gaming man who lost all his money and most of his health in those excesses of the club Arthur did (and still effectually does) belong to; how he made various efforts at reformation which his 'friends' there overbore; how he recovered and fell and finally with a superhuman struggle managed to forswear all intemperance in favour of a restorative marriage:

' "But now I see what it is that keeps me back, and what's wanted to save me; and I'd compass sea and land to get it— only I'm afraid there's no chance." And he sighed as if his heart would break.

' "What is it, Lowborough?" said I, thinking he was fairly cracked at last.

' "A wife," he answered; "for I can't live alone, because my own mind distracts me, and I can't live with you, because you take the devil's part against me."

' "Who—I?"

' "Yes—all of you do—and you more than any of them, you know. But if I could get a wife, with fortune enough to pay off my debts and set me straight in the world—"

' "To be sure," said I.

' "And sweetness and goodness enough," he continued, "to make home tolerable, and to reconcile me to myself, I think I should do yet. I shall never be in love again, that's certain; but perhaps that would be no great matter, it would enable me to choose with my eyes open—and I should make a good husband in spite of it; but could any one be in love with me?—that's the question. With your good looks and powers of fascination" (he was pleased to say), "I might hope; but as it is, Huntingdon, do you think anybody would take me—ruined and wretched as I am?"

' "Yes, certainly."

' "Who?"

' "Why, any neglected old maid, fast sinking in despair, would be delighted to—"

' "No, no," said he—"it must be somebody that I can love."

' "Why, you just said you never could be in love again!"

' "Well, love is not the word—but somebody that I can like. I'll search all England through, at all events!" he cried, with a sudden burst of hope, or desperation. "Succeed or fail, it will be better than rushing headlong to destruction at that d——d club: so farewell to it and you. Whenever I meet you on honest ground or under a Christian roof, I shall be glad to see you; but never more shall you entice me to that devil's den!" ' (Ch. 22)

Lowborough's highest dreams are exceeded in the event by his gaining Annabella Wilmot's hand in marriage: for she is a very lovely heiress who professes mutual devotion (though in fact she weds the bankrupt peer only for his title), and he adores her. This, on his side happy, wedding affirms and consolidates all his reformation; and it is something at least that he has many months of total physical and moral repair from it before learning—what nearly drives him to kill himself—that the habit of flirtation between her and Arthur Huntingdon is no social flippancy but their relationship is adulterous.

His character has strengthened through these ordeals however, and he becomes a figure deeply impressive as well as moving when he rises—a man for whom living is now a torment from which he longs to be released—even above the relief of fighting a duel with his rival; though of course that exposes him, in Hattersley's terms, to be grumbled at as a 'white-livered fool'. (' "No!" ' he has just exclaimed, 'with deep determined emphasis. "Though I hate him from my heart, and should rejoice at any calamity that could befall him, I'll leave him to God; and though I abhor my own life, I'll leave that, too, to Him that gave it." ')

The darkness that follows is a terrible one.

> She [Annabella] and Lord Lowborough [Helen confides to her Diary] occupied the apartments next to mine. I know not how she passed the night, but I lay awake the greater part of it listening to his heavy step pacing monotonously up and down his dressing-room, which was nearest my chamber. Once I heard him pause and throw something out of the window with a passionate ejaculation; and in the morning, after they were gone, a keen-bladed clasp-knife was found on the grass-plot below; a razor, likewise, was snapped in two and thrust deep into the cinders of the grate, but partially corroded by the decaying embers. So strong had been the temptation to end his miserable life, so determined his resolution to resist it. (Ch. 38)

The present critic is not hymning the praises of suffering, the least touch of which sends him whizzing round any available space screaming (and screaming 'It's not fair!'— often far from accurately). The matter is otherwise. This book showing us soul-growths, and the terrible prices they come at, as well as deteriorations, intimates that such choices—heroic, difficult, redemptive—are open to us all. Screwtape would have his own comment on this:

> Do not be deceived, Wormwood. Our cause is never more in danger, than when a human, no longer desiring, but still

intending, to do our Enemy's will, looks round upon a universe from which every trace of Him seems to have vanished, and asks why he has been forsaken, and still obeys.[1]

Hattersley instances improvement in another species. At a critical moment Helen Huntingdon turns on him and shows how he has misvalued his wife.

> '. . . Since you will mistake her silence for indifference, come with me, and I'll show you one or two of her letters—no breach of confidence, I hope, since you are her other half.'
> He followed me into the library. I sought out and put into his hands two of Milicent's letters: one dated from London, and written during one of his wildest seasons of reckless dissipation; the other in the country, during a lucid interval. The former was full of trouble and anguish; not accusing him, but deeply regretting his connection with his profligate companions, abusing Mr. Grimsby and others, insinuating bitter things against Mr. Huntingdon, and most ingeniously throwing the blame of her husband's misconduct on to other men's shoulders. The latter was full of hope and joy, yet with a trembling consciousness that this happiness would not last; praising his goodness to the skies, but with an evident, though but half-expressed wish, that it were based on a surer foundation than the natural impulses of the heart, and a half-prophetic dread of the fall of that house so founded on the sand,—which fall had shortly after taken place, as Hattersley must have been conscious while he read. (Ch. 42)

Taught by bitter experience, Helen is by then the most chastened realist, so that though in fact the shafts go home, at the right time and place, and this episode triggers off his amendment to become a good paterfamilias who before was a fellow 'tempter' with Grimsby & Co., she has sense a-plenty not to count on it in the 'now', the present tense of her narration.

> Shortly after they took their leave. They are now gone on a visit to Hattersley's father. After that they will repair to their country home. I hope his good resolutions will not fall through, and poor Milicent will not be again disappointed. Her last letter was full of present bliss, and pleasing anticipations for the future; but no particular temptation has yet occurred to put his virtue to the test. Henceforth, however, she will doubtless be somewhat less timid and reserved, and he more kind and thoughtful. (Ibid.)

When the book takes a last look at him, in the event, it is a happy family, now securely happy, of which he is the head.

The trouble with Huntingdon, in contradistinction to these gents, is he has little latent strength of character, and that little has long been enfeebled by perpetual self-indulgence. As anyone can tell who has ever worked in an 'institution', let alone cast an eye over the broad bosom of Mother Earth, there just are *some* people thus weak-willed; and what Helen's husband, with his money and idleness, fatally lacks is the iron discipline of some necessarily continent method of life, a regimen of compelled sanity. Relative poverty from early on might have done this for him (though one recalls, with misgiving, Branwell Brontë's failure to make good from a house where funds were visibly short), or alternatively a military or legal or other career requiring regular lucid thinking on important avocations. Given the failure of such things to be the conditions of his life, it rests with him to take a grip and organize his existence rationally: a step which he never takes.

The unlikelihood of his ever bringing his personality and *modus vivendi* into order and domestic peace is the first thrust of Anne Brontë's thematic interests here. It was arrogant folly in her heroine which persuaded her she could 'convert' the man she loved out of his faults into some being superior to what she really had evidence for thinking him.

She is given sufficient proofs early and late in their courtship dealings of his real personality, and has been guilty of wilful blindness on the subject. First of all, in Chapter 18, he is ungenerous and indelicate in handling her drawings of him as he does; then, when he knows she loves him, he flirts with Miss Wilmot (Ch. 19). In Chapter 20 he gives earnest of his worldliness in promising to deceive her aunt as to the piety of his character; and during the autumn of their betrothal announces his own, almost the worst, part in Lowborough's former prodigalities.

Here we touch an artistic weakness. It hardly seems plausible that Huntingdon would confess so much of his bad past to the rich fiancée he wants, no less for herself than her money, at a time so dangerous to his security. Yet we would credit the lengthy self-revelation of depravity which Chapter 22 consists in, if we felt something more substantial still: the force of his attraction for Helen in the first place. A key Freudian slip in the whole authorial lapse which is this vein of *The Tenant* is to be found in the next chapter:

> At this he only laughed and kissed my hand, calling me a sweet enthusiast. Then taking off his hat, he added: 'But look here, Helen—what can a man do with such a head as this?'
> The head looked right enough, but when he placed my hand on the top of it, it sunk in a bed of curls, rather alarmingly low, especially in the middle.
> 'You see I was not made to be a saint,' said he, laughing. 'If God meant me to be religious, why didn't He give me a proper organ of veneration?'

We are not here bothered with phrenology, another of the nineteenth century's exploded sciences, but with the fact that so newly married as she is, the loving Helen can speak like that about her spouse's cranium. He may look like the Missing Link for all we know; yet in her narration at such a juncture his every feature should figure as ideally assimilated to her notions of male beauty. There is this general failure in Anne Brontë's prose to convey something her poetry and reasoning regularly declare she herself experienced: the erotic charge which colours one individual's awareness of another when amorous love is in the case.

As in a milder version of *Clarissa*, the author sets up with subtle painstaking and success all the conditions for Helen Lawrence's falling, despite sensible advice and hard evidence, for such a 'scapegrace' against her own intelligence's promptings (which are themselves, in the chapters—17–21—describing the 'courtship', suitably represented), and marrying him against her own misgivings and uneasiness; but that Huntingdon is an agent of transfiguring light, energy, excitement in Helen's life at that period (or later) remains mere allegation. We are never made to feel it.

We well appreciate how a lively vigorous-minded girl like her needs to escape from the earlier round of her existence. The cheerless rectitude of her aunt's establishment, the lack of good company in her uncle, would be dismal enough of themselves, but to them is now added an offer of marriage from an ugly boorish middle-aged bore (the deliberately named Mr. Boarham) who is deducibly to be only the first in a string of such oppressions—since her guardians heavily urge the match upon her—just when she is entering upon the hopes and excitement of 'coming out' into young adult society. Yet Arthur Hunting-don's attraction remains a token which we have to pass like a counterfeit under the attention of our credence. We inevitably remark to ourselves, 'His appeal for Helen Lawrence is not half so well incarnated by the author as her disquietudes respecting his character'; so that the match seems far from the all but inevitable thing that in life actually it would have been.

This may be simply a failure of young art, attempting to describe from without love unworthily bestowed—in that sense a mere gap in the author's own conscious experience. We would set it down thus, save that the same flaw characterizes Anne Brontë's handling of the relations between Annabella Wilmot (by then Lowborough) and Helen's husband later. We are told they are a good-looking trivial-hearted vivacious couple, and witness their high animal spirits: yet the interest each awakens in the other is something we have to accept as a *donnée*, like a liaison testified to by a series of unimpeachable witnesses in some sordid court-case, but unknown to the jury's individual observation. The magnetism in those two persons' mutual regard is not conveyed by whatever authorial means.

When we put beside these lapses the failure to represent an erotic impulse on either side of the Agnes Grey–Edward Weston relationship in her earlier novel, we may well decide that there was a gap in Anne Brontë's equipment, whether of art or sensibility—probably both, since it seems the function of an inhibitedness in rendering feelings between the sexes, not a failure on her own part ever to know such sensations herself. Here of course her sister Charlotte plays her off the field. But I cannot wish that our author had either thrown down her pen or stuck to tasks (such as *Agnes Grey*) where the amorous element in human motivations signified little amongst their terms of debate. On the contrary, one of the very proofs of the youngest Brontë's greatness is that, after a wholly successful novel of courtship, she undertook this study of a marriage. They were, agreed, different enterprises—for *Agnes Grey* deals with a couple happily paired—yet also they are allied, since it is in the nature of a great artist (it is one of his or her hallmarks), having albeit produced one kind of perfection, to readjust the focus *and progress*.

In this undertaking—a much larger canvas than her previous publication, and treating an experience of which in one aspect (matrimony itself) she had no first-hand knowledge—Anne Brontë was being creatively daring in the right mode. We have here no simple case of a writer who does not know her limitations. When the newly wed Helen Huntingdon describes her honeymoon trip to the Continent, the author finds a good reason for not depicting Paris and Rome (Ch. 23); and we may recall that while Mr. Brontë, Charlotte and Emily went abroad, Anne never did. She makes a clever virtue here, all substantiating her theme, out of necessity—the need of not being called upon to give a fresh unique series of foreign impressions that she has not had herself, and avoiding sounding like disguised quotations from guide-books or others' recollections:

> The first instance he gave was on the occasion of our bridal tour. He wanted to hurry it over, for all the continental scenes were already familiar to him: many had lost their interest in his eyes, and others had never had anything to lose. The consequence was, that after a flying transit through part of France and part of Italy, I came back nearly as ignorant as I went, having made no acquaintance with persons and manners, and very little with things, my head swarming with a motley confusion of objects and scenes; some, it is true, leaving a deeper and more pleasing impression than others, but these embittered by the recollection that my emotions had not been shared by my companion, but that, on the contrary, when I had expressed a particular interest in anything I saw or desired to see, it had been displeasing to him, inasmuch as it proved that I could take delight in anything disconnected with himself.
>
> As for Paris, we only just touched at that, and he would not give me time to see one-tenth of the beauties and interesting objects of Rome. He wanted to get me home, he said, to have me all to himself, and to see me safely installed as the mistress of Grassdale Manor, just as single-minded, as naïve, and piquante as I was; and as if I had been some frail butterfly, he expressed himself fearful of rubbing the silver off my wings by bringing me into contact with society, especially that of Paris and Rome; and,

moreover, he did not scruple to tell me that there were ladies in both places that would tear his eyes out if they happened to meet him with me.

What Anne Brontë has used *is* first-hand, her observation of the 'polish'—or much rather, the patina—which adheres to an intelligent personality simply from the fact of having travelled in other lands and cultures; the different kind of awareness, self-possession and confidence—the *education* in short—which characterizes a perceptive woman who has crossed the English Channel on any excursion longer than a literal day-trip. So much as that her sisters' voyagings *could* directly afford her. Helen writes her narrative as a self-contained, experienced-sounding lady, who actually, we begin to realize, is still little more, in emotional terms, than a giddy teenager—*viz.* the banal manner of her first big matrimonial quarrel (in Ch. 24 following). The patina of foreign experience confers much but not omnicompetent wisdom.

No, we are here in presence of no essential artistic *manque* or of abilities too radically flawed. On the contrary, it is worth noting the marvellous management of her story which characterizes this author's achievement. From the very beginning, for instance, there is always a mystery to lead us on and inward: something to wonder at, some sinister or other stimulus of expectation. First it is the past history of 'Helen Graham'; then, when that begins to be revealed, the progress of her marriage—how, since we started the story six years before *it* began, that union has worked out in the meanwhile; and so on. Yet Pelion is not piled upon Ossa; we do not throw down the text in disgust after page 200 or wherever crying 'Enough of this trifling! Mysteries swarm too thick upon one another either to reflect real life or to let me feel other than sorely teased, whether by poor or mischievous craftsmanship.' I find it impressive rather than otherwise, that having penned a novel of courtship, Anne Brontë extends her frame and takes up a tale of wedlock. If she had been of the minor order of creators, she would either have set her hand to an ambitious scheme that was wholly beyond her powers and, in the execution, an approved fiasco; or she would have stayed at her *point de départ* to repeat herself. At particular moments *her* wisdom speaks out directly:

'. . . Keep both heart and hand in your own possession, till you see good reason to part with them; and if such an occasion should never present itself, comfort your mind with this reflection, that though in single life your joys may not be very many, your sorrows, at least, will not be more than you can bear. . . .'

(Ch. 41)

Thus Helen Huntingdon to the young bewildered Esther Hargrave when her advice is sought upon the subject. The speaker is admittedly wedlock-chastened and scarred but that last phrase is oracular. Those words, cool and gravely judicious as they are, ring (not least in their context) like Dr. Johnson's best prose or T. S. Eliot's most mature verse as with the deeply weighed experience, the poignantly achieved authority of a sensitive mind's lifetime. And they are all the more worth remembering, therefore, when literary legend obtrudes: we have them from the same Anne Brontë who is known to biographical art as a desperately shy wallflower that 'never told her love', pined for him from a distance, had possibly her affections somewhat trifled with by a man she may have overrated, and altogether figures as a sort of perpetual adolescent.

So: let us accept the bag of gold the author hands us and wink at its one false coin as 'twere valid; taking the amorous entanglements of the tale (all plausible that they would be better realized) for actually achieved which are little more than stated. This is not a desperate concession, the imaginative jump is a small one, violating no fundamental principles of human action as it does (rather, co-operating with likelihood); and, once made, it brings us out upon solid ground. *The Tenant of Wildfell Hall* works well as intended: a useful fable of warning against what may be the most frequent matrimonial mistake— that of one party to a marriage entering it, ill-advisedly out of a compulsive affection, with the intent of 'reforming' or changing some major aspect of the other's nature. Anne Brontë's theme and demonstration are wholly adequate: though other individuals can put in a useful oar from time to time, in fundamentals we only convert ourselves, and if the necessary choices be not accomplished by us they never will come to pass.

*   *   *

The high order of intellection we are here dealing with has, however, all its trump-cards yet to play. For *The Tenant* gives us a much larger treatment of human life than that summary implies; and punishes us with a greatly more inclusive vision of Man's situation than to point only those morals—radical truths and hard enough of digestion as they are. What it finds, almost uniquely in our prose fiction, a means of providing is a method of portraying life's unknowability, its (from the mortal point of view) patternless Pattern.

One of the few fundamental disabilities of any artistic treatment of life—but it is serious—is that of its nature art almost inevitably confers romance upon, and infers aptness in, every human fate with which it deals. E. M. Forster got so exasperated by this function of the Novel as a form that with careful preparation but apparent suddenness he would kill off a major character half way through *his* stories. In *Aspects of the Novel* he laments what is effectually a symptom of this deadliest feature of the species:

> . . . they go off at the end. . . . The characters have been getting out of hand, laying foundations and declining to build on them afterwards, and now the novelist has to labour personally, in order that the job may be done to time. He pretends that the characters are acting for him. He keeps mentioning their names and using inverted commas. But the characters are gone or dead.[2]

The process is nearly fatal because so questionably true to life. I am not now myself thinking of the gap between, say, the 'happy ever after' which a writer alleges for his creations at the end of a celebrative comedy and the mingled yarn which at the best life is going to be for practically any sublunary creature— that is an aesthetic problem of a much smaller order. The 'they lived happily (or for that matter, they died miserably) ever after' conclusion can have poetic, i.e. philosophic, essential truth. What the novelist's enterprise does so drastically entail is the implication that in all the flux of experience his/her characters' lives are proceeding along *significant* lines, however brutal or demeaning their individual trajectories.

Zola's *Germinal* will exemplify this. It is so written as to eschew, as much as manageably, having a 'hero' or 'heroine' while holding our interest nonetheless; yet the young couple who come nearest to filling those roles, Étienne and Catherine, when they perish in the mine at the close, or, through all their earlier vicissitudes, we scarcely think to say 'This is/was not their inevitable fate. They could have taken a hundred other turnings when choice did present itself at all, and the endings those elections led to would have been aesthetically no less valid.' Yet that great novel's power is founded not only on its author's 'density of specification', so that the industrial machine into which the shown human mass is fed eventually steams in our very nostrils as an enormous living beast; it derives also from the detachment conferred by Zola's earnest Socialist Materialism. The 'Naturalism', by the light of which he wrote, was determinist in essentials but not human particulars. He believes in the eventual collapse of the capitalist-industrial system, and chooses proleptically to foreshadow this in a scene of great force: but he does not infer fixed predestinations (of endings) for this and that individual in a given French coal-field. Yet in answering to *Germinal*'s philosophical-imaginative integrity, the conclusion press-gangs the *jeune premiers* I have spoken of into offering themselves up, as instanced destinies, for the significance implicit in the whole; and in that sense at least their lives become 'meaning-full', not random concatenations of experience which just, one day, end. Query therefore: have they not been betrayed, or Existence's own character de-natured?

Anne Brontë's method clumps its way through this one with the insouciance of a time-travelling brontosaur from a primordial era, transported to a tropical rain-forest and stepping through the solitary hut in its track. It is all to the point because the question must at some stage be put—have Helen and Arthur Huntingdon done each other any good, in the long or short term?

On the evidence *he* has certainly not benefited from this marriage: his character collapses pretty well as fast as it can, and with it his health. The novel several times hints directly, as well as continuously implying by the very nature of its subject-matter, that he would have been much better off either a financially poorer man or one otherwise compelled to an occupation.

MARCH 25TH.—Arthur is getting tired—not of me, I trust, but of the idle, quiet life he leads—and no wonder, for he has so few sources of amusement: he never reads anything but newspapers and sporting magazines; and when he sees me occupied with a book, he won't let me rest till I close it. In fine weather he generally manages to get through the time pretty well, but on rainy days, of which we have had a good many of late, it is quite painful to witness his ennui. (Ch. 24)

Suppose all the women with fortunes in the world conspired not to wed such types, would they not be happier here and hereafter?

As for Helen herself, what it has corrected in her of spiritual vanity has been scoured away at high cost: she is a woman much changed in appearance by the end—and one who has almost lost the gift of knowing how to be happy at all, let alone spontaneously. If wiser, she is a lot sadder. What ultimate *point* does her marriage to him have? Her education? Yes but her original sin was not so grave that life's lesser knocks would not have whittled it away: we view there vanity in a relatively venial degree and artless sort. So arguably, had her uncle's home been less oppressive or her aunt one degree more persuasive, all this misery would not have overtaken her—and we shall not know any certain answer to the question whether it has brought spiritual health in its wake.

For two reasons. On the most charitable consideration Arthur Huntingdon's soul breathes no odour of sanctity as it quits this world: we do not feel any degree of transfiguring comfort, albeit (as to kind) *in* Dostoyevskyan *extremis*, at that dreadful scene. Even on a Universalist view, Huntingdon must wander through purgatorial fires of much fiercer and longer duration than his failure to marry an attractive heiress would have necessitated. And in this world the lady's judgement hardly figures to our imaginations as now more certain of making good resolves for her future. That is illustrated by Gilbert Markham's part in the novel.

We are taking subtle measures here. I am not derogating by one iota from the acknowledgement made before, that the novel deserves tribute as a fine study, thoroughly 'deterministic' if you will, in the logic of personality working its own way through to destruction or improvement. As soon as Helen and

Arthur marry, they are doomed: and in precisely the way we are given to observe. But recognizing the book's high achievement in that regard does not suppress this other question that the action insistently prompts: Suppose the heroine, on an impulse of decisive doubt, had said 'No' and been hurried off out of his reach when Huntingdon proposed; or that proofs incontro-vertible had reached her of his licentiousness in former time, as depravity serious and far from easily eradicable? She has not been so deaf and blind that she would have failed to repudiate the match on such grounds as that:

> 'You think, then, that he is a virtuous, well-conducted young man?'
> 'I know nothing positive respecting his character. I only know that I have heard nothing definite against it—nothing that could be proved, at least; and till people can prove their slanderous accusations, I will not believe them.' (Ch. 17)

The real upshot of these questions, which the novel of itself (not my waywardness) provokes, rests with its portrait *in toto* of human choices: they are blind elections made in an anarchic void.

The 'enclosing narrator' of the piece, the young gentleman farmer with whom we began, presents a self which gradually disquiets our nerves. Terry Eagleton has well characterized the early impact of Markham and his household:

> There is a gossipy, self-indulgent, complacent domesticity about the Markham family which is intended to put the reader on guard: [quotes from paragraphs 5 and 6 of Chapter 1]. . . . There follows a cosy scene in which the family take tea, super-vised by a mother ('that honoured lady') who is described with the same mixture of ironic jocoseness and covert sentimentalism. The whole tableau is calculatedly fussy; and the effect is under-scored by Gilbert's brother Fergus, whose boorishness is meant to offer a sardonic contrast with his delicately-minded kin. . . . Gilbert himself is foolishly sentimental; and since it is he and not the novel who maintains that, though 'a little bit spoiled by [his] mother and sister, and some other ladies of [his] acquaintance', he is 'by no means a fop', we can take it that the book, in allowing him to protest too much, has serious reservations about his character. He is touchy and overbred, full of rhetorical gestures and gallant clichés, alternating between tender idealizations and

bursts of histrionic wrath. He is, in fact, emotionally infantile, ready to 'stamp with vexation' when his candle won't light, falling easily into self-pitying misanthropy as a rejected lover, quick to inflict grotesque violence on Helen's brother Mr. Lawrence.[3]

That however typifies only half the early materials in question. We also respond to the felt and shown homeliness of the farm, the warmth and good management of its kitchen-life, to Mrs. Markham (senior) as a proper domestic economist who has brought up her children on serious and valid principles of conduct (in the main). We are not introduced to a family of monsters or a spawning-ground for depravity.

Nevertheless Gilbert Markham is not sufficiently far off from the monster-condition for our comfort. As the action progresses we allow much to his hectic feelings of, first, unrequited and then frustrated love; but once he has read through the whole terrible saga which Helen Huntingdon's diary unfolds and which includes graphic descriptions, when all is said, of the torments of several other people as well as her own, we feel our tolerance has been misplaced. Indeed exasperation becomes decisive as we note that his first extended reaction to the whole is self-regard and concern about how *he* now figures in the imagination of the woman by whom he is obsessed. It is appalling that in a sense he cares for her so little intrinsically, that he can turn from the first revelation of the length and breadth of her recent and current miseries to such trampling egotism:

NOVEMBER 3RD.—I have made some further acquaintance with my neighbours. The fine gentleman and beau of the parish and its vicinity (in his own estimation, at least) is a young . . .

Here it ended. The rest was torn away. How cruel, just when she was going to mention me! for I could not doubt it was your humble servant she was about to mention, though not very favourably, of course. I could tell that, as well by those few words as by the recollection of her whole aspect and demeanour towards me in the commencement of our acquaintance. Well! I could readily forgive her prejudice against me, and her hard thoughts of our sex in general, when I saw to what brilliant specimens her experience had been limited.

Respecting me, however, [etc., etc.]. . . .

(Ch. 44, final emphasis added)

He then flies to Wildfell Hall and devotes all his energies to increasing his mistress's burdens in mind and spirit—with long and harrowing arguments against the dictates of her reason and conscience at a time (after all) when she might expect just a little aghast sympathy from the only human being to whom she has confided the whole history of her most unhappy marriage in the toils of which she has to struggle yet (Ch. 45). He next goes to make a very inadequate and churlish apology to Mr. Lawrence for having practically (and without just cause, let us recall) killed him (even if Lawrence had been Mrs. 'Graham's' paramour and not her brother). The next chapters—though interspersed with lengthy epistolary accounts at first, from Mrs. Huntingdon to her brother, of her husband's final decline—are told in the main from Markham's point of view and, self-regarding as they are, they show sufficient civility, genuineness of devotion and decency of comportment on his part for us not to despair of the marriage which, years after its event, he announces at the end.

But his character, thus embodied, gives us pause to think. By how near a margin has Helen Lawrence come to making once again a disastrous match? We feel all the more uncertain about the answer, given the book's method—which is for Markham to present himself. *He* says how happy they all are, his wife and children, in the two-decades-later season of 'June 10th, 1847': but what might Helen's journal, her innermost confession, reveal, were it confided once more to us? Surely nothing like the exquisite horror and anguish she knew with Huntingdon; yet how can life be easy with a hysterical egotist who always bullyingly insists on having his own way? Presumably it is not all carefree fulfilment, even with one brought up in a manner and on principles very different from her former spouse's. Markham can say and elucidate much, but he never manages to explain the mystery of Lawrence's sustained coolness towards him in the latter phases of the story and the role of that future brother-in-law—a virtuous man who all along has shown he is solely concerned with his sister's own interests—in doing everything this side of fair play to inhibit and prevent Helen's second courtship. Which mystery is no conundrum if you look at Gilbert Markham through the eyes of a truly caring honest broker.

Yet despite her brother's scant approbation, what else is she to do, the widow of Grassdale Manor? After her husband's death she makes her suitor wait a long time (some fourteen months) before re-marrying; and she has cause enough to take the step. The alternative is to leave her little son, now growing up, fatherless; to become a sort of dried-up old maid, still young though she is in her tale of years; and to refuse the addresses of a man to whom she is attracted, in a world where there is not so much social mobility or choice.

For what the novel also manages to include in its compass is the strenuous nature of travel in the 1820s (before the railroads revolutionized this); and the dependent fact that if you are a middle-class person living out in the country, you meet few other individuals with an equal degree of education—with manners and converse that you can share. It is weary work for Markham travelling in his desperation (Chs. 51–2) at the fastest available speeds to reach Staningley, a real (and in those days very rural) place near Pudsey in West Yorkshire, from his own establishment elsewhere in the North country (probably near the East Riding's coast and proximity to Scarborough as I suspect the author of quoting the different 'Ridings' of those days as separated shires in her narrative).

Yet the alternative is unappealing. If you choose to stay in London, the bright lights, the whirl of company may dazzle and give false impressions. Helen Lawrence was badly bitten that way in the capital the first time around. She is twice shy of it—especially as a yet greater 'catch' of an inheritrix—now. At least with Gilbert Markham she knows she has been fallen in love with by someone who did so at her fortune's lowest ebb when she was a poor outcast. Should she hand her card about metropolitan society after the term of her widowhood's mourning, how much could she be sure about the sincerity of new proposals made to her there?

*   *   *

In the back of her prayer-book Anne Brontë one day pencilled the words 'sick of mankind and their disgusting ways'.[4] It is a sweeping comment and obviously cannot represent the whole of her reaction (as it were, forever) to the human experiment. If it had, she would not have written everything else we inherit from her. Yet it brings us back to one of the problematic cruxes of Helen Huntingdon's career in *The Tenant*. To what extent is her experience of society inclusive enough? Gilbert Markham assumes she has had unusual ill-luck with his 'Well, I could readily forgive her prejudice against me, and her hard thoughts of our sex in general, when I saw to what brilliant specimens her experience had been limited.'

How limited, however, *is* her experience? On one view, very much so. Women do in ordinary life meet wholesome members of the opposite sex, marry them and find themselves conducting their existences thereafter with beings considerably superior in character to either Arthur Huntingdon or the gentleman farmer with whom this heroine is settled when the tale concludes.

The impression, all the same, of a social world where choices are not many and brilliant is amplified by the case of Esther Hargrave.

Mature indeed is the depiction of this personality. As in real life, so with Helen's neighbouring young friend in this novel; when we first get to know her she is fairly dislikeable: a pert young officious, thrusting girl who will not take hints, who is generally insensitive—and whose conversation jars, rushing in where even an ordinary quantity of tact would have the sense not so much as to tiptoe. Gradually Helen's better opinion (than ours) becomes vindicated—and in that process, of course, the novelist also gains the effect of our being the surer that we are not witnessing, in the principal protagonist, some straightforward fool of a woman who is merely of the undiscriminative type always and inevitably to bring down sufferings like rain upon her head.

Esther's loud boisterous cheer finally shows for the function of an unself-confident loneliness. She is the most feeling female member imprisoned in a family dominated by a snobbish match-making mother—and is also put through the '*Clarissa*-syndrome'.

July 29th.—Mrs. Hargrave and her daughter are come back from London. Esther is full of her first season in town; but she is still heart-whole and unengaged. Her mother sought out an excellent match for her, and even brought the gentleman to lay his heart and fortune at her feet; but Esther had the audacity to refuse the noble gifts. He was a man of good family and large possessions, but the naughty girl maintained he was old as Adam, ugly as sin, and hateful as—one who shall be nameless.

'But, indeed, I had a hard time of it,' said she: 'mamma was very greatly disappointed at the failure of her darling project, and very, very angry at my obstinate resistance to her will, and is so still; but I can't help it. And Walter, too, is so seriously displeased at my perversity and absurd caprice, as he calls it, that I fear he will never forgive me—I did not think he could be so unkind as he has lately shown himself. But Milicent begged me not to yield, and I'm sure, Mrs. Huntingdon, if you had seen the man they wanted to palm upon me, you would have advised me not to take him too.'

'I should have done so whether I had seen him or not,' said I; 'it is enough that you dislike him.'

'I knew you would say so; though mamma affirmed you would be quite shocked at my undutiful conduct. You can't imagine how she lectures me: I am disobedient and ungrateful; I am thwarting her wishes, wronging my brother, and making myself a burden on her hands. I sometimes fear she'll overcome me after all. I have a strong will, but so has she, and when she says such bitter things, it provokes me to such a pass that I feel inclined to do as she bids me, and then break my heart and say, "There, mamma, it's all your fault!" '

'Pray don't!' said I. 'Obedience from such a motive would be positive wickedness, and certain to bring the punishment it deserves. Stand firm, and your mamma will soon relinquish her persecution; and the gentleman himself will cease to pester you with his addresses if he finds them steadily rejected.'

'Oh no! mamma will weary all about her before she tires herself with her exertions; and as for Mr. Oldfield, she has given him to understand that I have refused his offer, not from any dislike of his person, but merely because I am giddy and young, and cannot at present reconcile myself to the thoughts of marriage under any circumstances: but by next season, she has no doubt, I shall have more sense, and hopes my girlish fancies will be worn away. So she has brought me home, to school me into a proper sense of my duty, against the time comes round again. Indeed, I believe she will not put herself to the expense of taking me up to London again, unless I surrender: she cannot afford to take me to town for pleasure and nonsense, she says, and it is not every rich gentleman that will consent to take me without a fortune, whatever exalted ideas I may have of my own attractions.' (Ch. 41)

The counsel which Helen offers her there, already quoted, rings as gold which has been tried in the fire, yet Esther's response is also unanswerable:

> 'So thinks Milicent; but allow me to say I think otherwise. If I thought myself doomed to old-maidenhood, I should cease to value my life. The thoughts of living on, year after year, at the Grove—a hanger-on upon mamma and Walter, a mere cumberer of the ground (now that I know in what light they would regard it), is perfectly intolerable; I would rather run away with the butler.' (Ibid.)

Who can hold out against a myriad of perpetual oppressions and a future of dwelling at home on sufferance, the recipient of grudged charity with every bite they take at meals? The economic position of a woman in that society at that time is an all-important issue in Esther's situation, as a previous chapter made plain with its rendering of the way Milicent Hargrave was bounced into dismal fretting with the admission of Hattersley's proposals (Ch. 25)—a man with whom *she* nearly spends a life of complete wretchedness.

The hard facts are that in her own case Esther has to marry and is intelligent enough to hold out against marrying where she does not love: 'But I cannot leave them [mamma and Walter] unless I get married, and I cannot get married if nobody sees me. I saw one or two gentlemen in London that I might have liked, but they were younger sons, and mamma would not let me get to know them—one especially, who I believe rather liked me—but she threw every possible obstacle in the way of our better acquaintance. . . .' (Ch. 41)

What it all amounts to is this:—We shall argue for the rest of mortal Time the question, how much these women have a sufficiently representative experience of human society, as to the chances and choices that come before them, given in that day their immobility, their political status etc.; and indeed, if

The Tenant had the respect which is its due, this topic would be the subject *in perpetuo* of regular lively debate among people concerned with imaginative literature—like the question, how much Henry James knew 'the best' in Victorian circles (the morally finest, intellectually most nutritive among the fortunate classes of his time).[5] Yet finally that is not the central issue. What crucially comes to the fore as we consider Helen Lawrence's persecutions, then the two Hargrave sisters', is that the individual, every individual in this world in any epoch, does not have enough guidance from the Fates wherewith to make the 'correct' decisions. Anne Brontë's demonstration is drastic by the very fact that she does not take up an extreme position on this point. It is not that guidelines are missing: Esther Hargrave's own substantial sense and virtue are here most ably seconded by the purgatorially purchased wisdom of the senior woman to whom she has intelligently turned for advice. It is rather that all advice, however profound and fully accepted, all experience however hard-won, can only just go so far (i.e. not far enough) in helping us make the right election about the next phase in our careers (where a choice offers), as Helen's case goes on to show.

Mrs. Huntingdon's eventual cautious decision to marry Gilbert Markham answers to the needs of her situation and personality, and with no reckless spirit or tell-tale haste; but leaving her at the end, we are far from certain that she is now a soul blissfully yoked in this world: an uncertainty which would doubtless also have been our response if we heard that Esther had flown off to marry some choice—however careful, on the limited evidence—among the 'one or two gentlemen' in London that '[she] might have liked' as a refuge from home. Helen herself there comments: '. . . but it is possible that if you married him, you might have more reason to regret it hereafter than if you married Mr. Oldfield. When I tell you not to marry without love, I do not advise you to marry for love alone: there are many, many other things to be considered.'

By all its tactics the novel represents the inescapable dilemma of human sapience, brings graphically home to us the truth of Matthew Arnold's words, but here applied to social relations:

for the world, which seems
To lie before us like a land of dreams,
So various, so beautiful, so new,
Hath really neither joy, nor love, nor light,
Nor certitude, nor peace, nor help for pain;
And we are here as on a darkling plain
Swept with confused alarms of struggle and flight,
Where ignorant armies clash by night.[6]

In Chapter 39 of *The Golden Bowl* Maggie Verver, tormented by her household of adulterous unions, is aware of its visiting priest conversing with Charlotte, her new young mother-in-law and rival, about

> some approach he would have attempted with her, that very morning perhaps, to the circumstance of an apparent detachment, recently noted in her, from any practice of devotion. He would have drawn from this, say, his artless inference—taken it for a sign of some smothered inward trouble and pointed, naturally, the moral that the way out of such straits was not through neglect of the grand remedy.

James's genial dismissal of Christianity there, as well as sorting with his own humanist's temperament of mid-nineteenth/early twentieth-century atheism, is actually amusing in its place. So little has the role of any Church or religious creed figured in the thinking of the four main personages whose all but incestuous affinities have crowded the canvas of a long book hitherto, that for a clergyman to offer 'a better wisdom, the jostle of the higher light, of heavenly help itself' (two paragraphs earlier) and to do so in his ignorance of the tensions beneath this fraught surface (though the narrator sets him down as, like the others here present at table, also quite capable of having an 'instinct, sharper than the expression of his face'), provokes mainly an apt chuckle. In *The Tenant of Wildfell Hall* 'the grand remedy' appears ever more solidly, as we read, the *fons et origo*, the focus and altar of the whole.

Its sphere is only too accurate a reflection of the one outside the book's covers—an organum in which even the best prepared and intentioned of us move about too much in worlds unrealized to make the choices which can offer ourselves and our fellow-creatures either happiness or secure foundations for virtue.

Now there are two possible responses to this. One is to live on a tip-and-run basis, hoping (with somewhat extortionate optimism) that the bad luck which overtook Helen Lawrence (and her husband, in a degree) and which visibly we can observe working its logics out in the lives of perhaps three-quarters of our acquaintance (if we look below the facades) somehow will not, miraculously, happen to wonderful us: because we are in a mystic manner sacrosanct and special, or at least far cleverer than anybody else we know; for the novel's demonstration relates not merely to marriage choices alone but to all taken directions where there are forked ways, alternative paths in a human track.

The other method is to look to the Unmoved Mover of the spheres wherein earthly change has its being, the Absolute Reality behind the transitory veil of this world's appearances.

Here Helen Lawrence's creed earns its right of emphasis from the fact that she herself, with all her faults clearly on her head before us, is a successful version of (say) the Jane Fairfax in *Emma* which Austen tried, and failed, to bring off. Unlike that earlier avatar Helen is not a starched prig of a preacher, even on occasion. She has Jane Fairfax's beauty, her artistic talent, searching intelligence, unorthodox behaviour, and reserve in all company except that of the man she fixes her affections upon—and likewise with him she is eager, self-giving and passionate. All this is derived not out of felt superiority to her human fellows—though there is a venial element of this in her youthfulness—so much as because she *is* so perceptive and alone (those things both together). No more than with Agnes Grey do we feel moved to protest when she waxes theological: for her utterances (as Eagleton noted in his commentary on the governess-heroine[7]) are not covert ways of exploiting people and working off spleen in Pharisaic fashion, resentments disguised as holiness. In that regard her speech is a perspicuous window through which shine the Christian beliefs that, given not just her own extremities but what they illustrate of the whole—our general—human predicament, become her only lifeline in a world where reality itself is committedly Anarchist.

Her good faith in this regard is exemplified in the exchange she has with Milicent Hargrave, by now unhappily married as

Mrs. Hattersley, on the subject with which her meditations
have begun the chapter in question (Ch. 32)—Esther's future
fate.

> OCTOBER 5TH.—Esther Hargrave is getting a fine girl. She is
> not out of the school-room yet, but her mother frequently brings
> her over to call in the mornings when the gentlemen are out,
> and sometimes she spends an hour or two in company with her
> sister and me, and the children; and when we go to the Grove, I
> always contrive to see her, and talk more to her than to any one
> else, for I am very much attached to my little friend, and so is
> she to me. I wonder what she can see to like in me though, for I
> am no longer the happy, lively girl I used to be; but she has no
> other society, save that of her uncongenial mother, and her
> governess (as artificial and conventional a person as that
> prudent mother could procure to rectify the pupil's natural
> qualities), and, now and then, her subdued, quiet sister. I often
> wonder what will be her lot in life, and so does she; but her
> speculations on the future are full of buoyant hope; so were
> mine once. I shudder to think of her being awakened, like me,
> to a sense of their delusive vanity. It seems as if I should feel her
> disappointment, even more deeply than my own. I feel almost
> as if I were born for such a fate, but she is so joyous and fresh,
> so light of heart and free of spirit, and so guileless and
> unsuspecting too. Oh, it would be cruel to make her feel as I feel
> now, and know what I have known!

The unhappy Mrs. Huntingdon is emphatic in not prejudging
the unattached young woman among them to cynical views:

> '... I wish [says Milicent] you would seriously impress it
> upon her, never, on any account, or for anybody's persuasion,
> to marry for the sake of money, or rank, or establishment, or
> any earthly thing, but true affection and well-grounded esteem.'
> 'There is no necessity for that,' said I, 'for we have had some
> discourse on that subject already, and I assure you her ideas of
> love and matrimony are as romantic as any one could desire.'
> 'But romantic notions will not do: I want her to have true
> notions.'
> 'Very right: but in my judgment, what the world stigmatises
> as romantic, is often more nearly allied to the truth than is
> commonly supposed; for, if the generous ideas of youth are too
> often over-clouded by the sordid views of after-life, that scarcely
> proves them to be false.'

Their discussion serves also to turn the central screw of the work: its registration of the future's unknowableness, the hapless near-impossibility of making secure choices for sanity, let alone happiness. But its generosity, of hope and goodwill towards one as yet unfettered for life to a tormenting partner, gives (I should have thought) almost any reader a high threshold of tolerance for the quotations from Scripture and the moralist's deductions therefrom with which Helen confronts her husband at one crisis after another.

As he lies dying, appalled at his approaching dissolution, his wife tries to rouse his spiritual faculties and to comfort him in one and the same strain of remonstrance:

> ' "But if you sincerely repent———"
> ' "I can't repent; I only fear."
> ' "You only regret the past for its consequences to yourself?"
> ' "Just so—except that I'm sorry to have wronged you, Nell, because you're so good to me."
> ' "Think of the goodness of God, and you cannot but be grieved to have offended Him."
> ' "What is God?—I cannot see Him or hear Him.—God is only an idea."
> ' "God is Infinite Wisdom, and Power, and Goodness—and LOVE; but if this idea is too vast for your human faculties—if your mind loses itself in its overwhelming infinitude, fix it on Him who condescended to take our nature upon Him, who was raised to heaven even in His glorified human body, in whom the fulness of the Godhead shines."
> 'But he only shook his head and sighed. Then, in another paroxysm of shuddering horror, he tightened his grasp on my hand and arm, and, groaning and lamenting, still clung to me with that wild, desperate earnestness so harrowing to my soul, because I know I cannot help him. I did my best to soothe and comfort him.
> ' "Death is so terrible," he cried, "I cannot bear it! You don't know, Helen,—you can't imagine what it is, because you haven't it before you! and when I'm buried, you'll return to your old ways and be as happy as ever, and all the world will go on just as busy and merry as if I had never been; while I———" He burst into tears.
> ' "You needn't let that distress you," I said; "we shall all follow you soon enough."

' "I wish to God I could take you with me now!" he exclaimed: "you should plead for me."

' "No man can deliver his brother, nor make agreement unto God for him," I replied: "It cost more to redeem their souls—it cost the blood of an incarnate God, perfect and sinless in Himself, to redeem us from the bondage of the evil one:—let Him plead for you."

'But I seem to speak in vain. He does not now, as formerly, laugh these blessed truths to scorn: but still he cannot trust, or will not comprehend them. He cannot linger long. He suffers dreadfully, and so do those that wait upon him. But I will not harass you with further details: I have said enough, I think [she is writing to her brother], to convince you that I did well to go to him.' (Ch. 49)

The problem however—the other major flaw of this novel— is that while Anne Brontë, and I and some other people, exactly believe what Helen Huntingdon there declares, 'these blessed truths' are not the speculum through which the world and its history are interpreted by nearly every English-reading person today. Consider the year *The Tenant* was written, or completed: 1848. Marx and Engels were publishing (in London) *The Manifesto of the Communist Party*: a classic state-ment of (post-Newtonian) materialism; Wagner was issuing his *Nibelung's Ring* poem and commencing its setting to music—which perhaps is (certainly in temper it harmonizes as) the profoundest statement of the Darwinian thesis: Evolu-tion, endless becoming, and maybe behind that, cyclical cosmic convulsions; Man as product of a 'god' so remote from anthropomorphic considerations as to have little in common with the attributes specifically alleged of the Christian Deity. The tenor of the age, the modern mind (*Der Ring des Nibelungen* significantly *antedates* publication of *The Origin of Species*) finds Helen's concluding apostrophe, quoted there above, far from inevitably accurate.

What is lacking under Anne Brontë's hand are the very means of proving her case. A novelist cannot conduct her enterprise as theological disputant: that is to fall between both functions; still less, simply as a philosopher inditing an essay, can she argue readers into a given set of beliefs because (a) all religious faith is a personal thing, a *donnée* (which may inhere early or late in a life) and (b)—it is the same point, largely— Christianity invites the individual into a personal unique relation with his Maker-Redeemer, not a series of deductions, like one of Euclid's theorems or the Constitution of The United States, which he is required, however warmly convinced, to sign.

If One has come back from the dead and yet we do not believe, how can even a great novelist writing at such a time as that, this all-representative date of the Modern Epoch, carry conviction into every breast? In this aspect *The Tenant* is 'only a story': and the non- or anti-religious will say 'a tall one at that'.

My own view of the role for the imaginative author in the modern era is that he/she may include specific promulgations of Christian doctrine or analyses of themes therein (*viz.* Dostoyevsky) as integers of his creations. But these must be incorporated in a narrative, a vision, which does not decisively *hinge* upon the reader's acceptance of the credo, or its essentials, for exertion of its appeal and empowering of its themes. Thus in large part we have the beauty of Shakespeare's process and the failure of the twentieth-century verse-dramatists. A very leading Shakespearian scholar once told me (himself an agnostic) that half a lifetime's study had persuaded him our greatest poet probably, on doctrinal questions, saw eye to eye with Hooker; and believers like myself will always feel a lump in their throats, catch their breath upon a warmth which we associate with active sympathy when we come upon his occasional excursus that pay magniloquent tribute to the Nazarene who is our all-in-all: near the opening of *Hamlet*, for instance—

> Some say that ever 'gainst that season comes
> Wherein our Saviour's birth is celebrated,
> The birth of dawning singeth all night long:
> And then, they say, no spirit dare stir abroad;
> The nights are wholesome; then no planets strike,
> No fairy takes, nor witch hath power to charm,
> So hallowed and so gracious is the time. (I, i)

Or still more impressive, the inspiration which leaps from the lips of the fierily impassionated Isabella in *Measure for Measure* when, albeit herself a very mixed-up young maiden, she pleads for her brother's life:

Why, all the souls that were were forfeit once;
And He that might the vantage best have took
Found out the remedy. How would you be,
If He, which is the top of judgement, should
But judge you as you are? O, think on that;
And mercy then will breathe within your lips,
Like man new made. (II, ii)

Those first two and a half lines contain 'conceits' which in profundity may match any one of Dante's or Donne's. (Is there something in *God's* self-denials we have overlooked, a vantage given up? And note how she utters a Boethian view of Time: 'all the souls that *were*'; we are suddenly pulled up into viewing the proceedings from the Christian's seventh heaven. It comes as a shock.) Yet you don't have to think of Shakespeare as possessed by this theology or any other to share, with all your fellow-attenders, the ample nutriment his work affords.

We are in problematic territory with *The Tenant*. Its matter is handled with perfect tact as far as that can go. Helen Huntingdon is an intelligent, worthwhile Christian young matron whose piety is not spurious or unattractive and whose faults, such as they are, precisely seem to us the consequences of her emotional inanitions. But all the positive side of the novel's 'message' hangs upon a credence in the reader, like unto this heroine's, of the 'blessed truths' she speaks.

Anne Brontë was in a cruel dilemma, every bit as much moral as artistic. If she did not, with her main protagonist, so pen her analysis of the mortal predicament and locate its refuge explicitly

> . . . There then! the Master,
> *Ipse*, the only one, Christ, King, Head:
> He was to cure the extremity where he had cast her;
>   Do, deal, lord it with living and dead;[8]

then she would be guilty of telling only half the human story and that in an age when the hungry sheep look up and are not fed. In her day and ours, as in the Corinth of St. Paul's generation, Occidental humanity's philosophical plight is desperate. Especially if you do take a Marxian, evolutionary or other materialist view of history, the individual's life becomes a nonsense between two endless voids; and about the life of the race, or the doings of the stars, one can only mouth abstract generalizations, essentially meaningless, where is scant comfort for the mind since it is there dealing with entities which are not, *as consciant, feeling entities.* ('What is Thought but an "I" thinking?' asked Coleridge. Quite; and what is a species, or its future, unless in the apperception of some other active living consciousness, but the particular individuals which all aggregate it?)

Metaphysically matters have looked up somewhat since then—indeed since 1905. Einsteinian physics debunk much of the post-Newtonian assumptions; and at this very time of writing Darwinism begins to totter on its pedestal, not from the shoves of Fundamentalists in the southern states of the U.S.A. so much as from ugly lunges of contemporary mathematics in the D.N.A. calculus.[9] It is telling that *still* (in 1983!) very little of these physics which actual scientists now believe is taught in the world's schools, and scarcely anything has penetrated—I mean since the Relativity theories were argued all those decades ago—the newspapers of any shore, though they enforce belief that we and all creatures are a-material and invisible in strictest (unimaginable but accurate) scientific fact: an equation which enfeebles one of the traditional cases against theism—that God fails to show Himself. The conspiracy of misinformation (our schoolchildren all studying old hat in their Physics classes), the failure in the public prints to reproduce the Einsteinian model through year after year, all goes to suggest that eras have their tempers of mind and until the *mood* changes people will not admit either new ideas or the evidence for them. Galileo had the same problem, in 1610, with some nice as well as nasty Papists.

Equally *The Tenant*'s author does not, because she cannot, enforce credit for her creed. What we are left with, for corporate agreement in the public areopagus, is a novel which mauls the rationalist's mode of life pretty nearly to death. Gilbert Markham's whole enterprise, in the life of Helen Huntingdon, gets more and more disturbing as we ponder it.

He reads for himself the history of Walter Hargrave's treatment of his lady-love: how that apparently devoted blade has in fact a very selfish kind of appetite for the mistress of Grassdale

Manor and persecutes her with attentions and offers of adultery which nearly drive her mad (e.g. Chs. 29 and 37). Indeed in Chapter 33 there is a sinister scene, almost out of Jacobean drama for its flavour but entirely lifelike and contemporaneously realized from Anne Brontë's part, in which Hargrave plays chess with his heavily oppressed hostess, and in a series of *double entendres* signifies that what they are gaming for is her honour. The sexual and religious punning reveals of itself how he values this relationship; as a game, a contest for a woman's virtue, a battle—not something in the service of her happiness.

> 'It is those bishops that trouble me,' said he; 'but the bold knight can overleap the reverend gentlemen,' taking my last bishop with his knight; 'and now, those sacred persons once removed, I shall carry all before me.'
> 'Oh, Walter, how you talk!' cried Milicent; 'she has far more pieces than you still.'
> 'I intend to give you some trouble yet,' said I; 'and perhaps, sir, you will find yourself checkmated before you are aware. Look to your queen.'

Yet having perused such episodes in her tormented life at Grassdale which these her Diary-pages reveal, Markham can actually then rush off to apply just the same screw himself— and it does not much mend the matter that he knows in this case his amorous feeling is reciprocated:

> She was silent. Her pale lips quivered, and her fingers trembled with agitation, as she nervously entwined them in the hair-chain to which was appended her small gold watch—the only thing of value she had permitted herself to keep. [Symbol of her honour, her self-respect?] I had said an unjust and cruel thing; but I must needs follow it up with something worse.
> 'But, Helen!' I began in a soft, low tone, not daring to raise my eyes to her face, 'that man is not your husband: in the sight of heaven he has forfeited all claim to———' She seized my arm with a grasp of startling energy.
> 'Gilbert, don't!' she cried, in a tone that would have pierced a heart of adamant. 'For God's sake, don't you attempt these arguments! No friend could torture me like this!' (Ch. 45)

To be fair, he does not revert to this theme again, and appreciates its baseness. Yet he hardly figures as offering *her* moral comfort, spiritual strengthening during their interview at this crucial juncture. Rather the other way about; and she is the one who has been through the most protracted sufferings, whose future is most involved in dreary doubt (she will have to go back to Huntingdon, he may live for a score of years more, and yet she cannot desire his death, especially after the life he has led and the condition to which he is reduced). Similarly, when we conclude our reading of the whole, we may ask 'But *why* has Markham written this history down?' and it comes at us with a shock that the undertaking is a mere self-indulgence: that he has no better motive than beguiling time.

By 'June 10th, 1847' he is a middle-aged man, less bustlingly active than theretofore and content to do his self-entertaining now in sedentary posture at a chair and desk. Often and again Helen notes in her record how one of her few satisfactions is that she can speak the whole truth about her married state to that confidant and not fear to have it seen by anyone else than herself. That she has made an exception, in the event, for her sole supporter amidst the community round Wildfell Hall, does her little discredit. If there were aught, in all this revelation, which needed urgently to be told, the long exposé would even so be legitimate perhaps, but nothing of the sort seems to be the case; and when the book concludes with the words

> We are just now looking forward to the advent of you and Rose, for the time of your annual visit draws nigh, when you must leave your dusty, smoky, noisy, toiling, striving city for a season of invigorating relaxation and social retirement with us.
> Till then, . . .

we may well draw in our breath at this documented delivery of so much private confidence—confidence not even merely orally bestowed when its recipient arrives.

For Gilbert Markham is publishing his own love's annals and his wife's journal, to his brother-in-law 'Halford', a man whom we do not meet but on whose sensibility of discretion we may have limited cause to rely simply from the very fact that he married Rose Markham in the first place. While *she* has appeared in the text (her brother's part of its inditing), Rose has figured to us as a gossip not beyond the reach of unworthy influences and companions:

111

'No,' returned she, hesitatingly—'but I've heard so much about her lately, both at the Wilsons' and the vicarage;—and besides. . . . (Ch. 11)

Yet in spite of all this we cannot decide merely that Helen Lawrence has erred again in her choice of a partner for life. She obviously finds Markham attractive—that is implied at several points; she needs to marry someone; his addresses are disinterested as regards her fortune; he has plied an honest trade in the world, proved himself at that, and believed in her when almost all the others of the vicinity where she was situated did not. His good faith and ardour may not improperly be rewarded with her devotion. We are just disconcerted by those other aspects of his nature I have animadverted, and rather gapingly *unsure*.

Such use of narrations which are like Chinese boxes one within another for certain of the novel's essential effects adds strength to Mr. Chitham's (and others') view that in various ways *The Tenant of Wildfell Hall* parodies, in criticizing, *Wuthering Heights*.[10] We know that Anne was at first dismayed, then philosophically resilient, under the discovery that she and Emily, in their early time inseparable twins in feeling and thought, had grown radically apart, as to their visions of life and correspondent ethos. The poem 'Self-Communion' (quoted in Chapter 2 of this study) tells us as much. Charlotte of her part in her *Editor's Preface to the New [1850] Edition of Wuthering Heights* confesses that one or other of them remonstrated with Emily during the composition of that novel:

> If the auditor of her work, when read in manuscript, shuddered under the grinding influence of natures so relentless and implacable, of spirits so lost and fallen; if it was complained that the mere hearing of certain vivid and fearful scenes banished sleep by night, and disturbed mental peace by day, Ellis Bell would wonder what was meant, and suspect the complainant of affectation.

Only a great artist's caring intelligent relatives can be so dangerously obtuse (for they have enough understanding of the case in question, enough common rhetoric and credit most to act the Devil's Advocate for the betrayal of his or her best inspiration). One thinks of how William James the philosopher spent half his life imploring his brother to write a different kind of novel from what he evolved after his earliest successes. Why will clever—or even stupid—families not learn the only lesson?—that where great art is in hand, it must go its own way; and if it is not great art, it does not matter anyhow. It will be lost soon enough amidst the dusty shelves of history's lumber-room.

What that avowal also strongly suggests is that they delivered their writings to one another viva voce after that nine o'clock evening hour at Haworth Parsonage when they would put away their employments and begin to pace round and round its parlour table; that they invited thereby comment and argued values with one another through the fictional media they were now preparing to publish, no less than they had collaborated in the Angrian and Gondalian inventions they had kept to themselves when their views of the world were more private and homogeneous. We glimpse a more intimate version of the Inklings' meetings at their Oxford pub during the 1930s and '40s. Whether the Brontë sisters took each other's works in intermitted draughts as they were composed (like Tolkien and Lewis and Dorothy Sayers etc.) and offered criticism *in medias res* or only heard the whole achievements upon completion, we can deduce a process almost of stichomythia between the two youngest siblings now back at home together, united on some issues and on others far apart, a debate taking place between Emily and Anne in 1847 and 1848 which is fully reflected in their mss. as delivered to the printer.

The mutually antagonistic emphases of Emily's Shelleyan pantheism and Anne's orthodox Christianity, richly illustrated as these are in their respective tales, do not need any heavy belabouring in this commentary. Walter Allen has memorably expressed the fineness with which *Wuthering Heights* is 'the complete bodying forth of an intensely individual apprehension of the nature of man and life'.[11] All I can offer in addition is this thought: that the laurels of the contest should not all go to one of England's greatest 'poetic' fictionists; for, in one sense that counts, Anne's *magnum opus* gives more guidance for living.

When we have fully exposed ourselves to Emily's novel in that grateful awake humility of attentiveness which is the only appropriate response (as to Shakespeare's work) if one wants to get the nourishment out of it that is there, one question remains: what can we do with the awareness of life which it actualizes?

Well the first answer is that the book's *raison d'être*, like any great work of art, *is* the vision it constitutes: that this is freestanding, validly self-existent, with the justification of a daffodil or a lagoon. Being a thoroughgoing Jamesian in my aesthetics of the Novel, I want to acknowledge immediately that that should be our principal avowal. I disagree with the Master in his estimates of this and that author and text (drastically in certain cases) of course: we all shall, from one another. Yet when he writes in his Preface of 1908 to *The Portrait of a Lady* 'The house of fiction has in short not one window, but a million', and goes on to expatiate upon the variety of the minds looking through its fenestration, he hymns the very value of the form:

> These apertures, of dissimilar shape and size, hang so, all together, over the human scene that we might have expected of them a greater sameness of report than we find. They are but windows at the best, mere holes in a dead wall, disconnected, perched aloft; they are not hinged doors opening straight upon life. But they have this mark of their own that at each of them stands a figure with a pair of eyes, or at least with a field-glass, which forms, again and again, for observation, a unique instrument, insuring to the person making use of it an impression distinct from every other. He and his neighbours are watching the same show, but one seeing more where the other sees less, one seeing black where the other sees white, one seeing big where the other sees small, one seeing coarse where the other sees fine. And so on, and so on; there is fortunately no saying on what, for the particular pair of eyes, the window may *not* open; "fortunately" by reason, precisely, of this incalculability of range. The spreading field, the human scene, is the "choice of subject"; the pierced aperture, either broad or balconied or slit-like and low-browed, is the "literary form"; but they are, singly or together, as nothing without the posted presence of the watcher—without, in other words, the consciousness of the artist. Tell me what the artist is, and I will tell you of what he has *been* conscious. Thereby I shall express to you at once his boundless freedom and his "moral" reference.

We need to subject ourselves to Emily Brontë's mind and view, in order to receive a rich extension of our human experience. Art exists to enlarge our consciousness—when it does so pleasingly we call it beauty—and battling against the staleness of custom it dislodges also the yoke of mental habit. The great artist is such a benefactor to his species precisely in the fact of working, to these ends, with the originality of his vision and the competence of its expression pulling together, to make available to us a new experience of the world which we would not have had from ourselves 'all on our own'.

Indeed, I will go further and confess that in my view ultimately Life itself is about having, is valid for offering, certain kinds of vision. Faced with the ultimate question 'Well we want a just society, yes of course, and the rest of the edenic thing as much as possible; but what even then is it all for?; what would be the point, even in an Earthly Paradise, of getting up in the morning, quaffing one's nectar and settling disputes amongst the feathered creation—what is the point of brushing one's teeth and going to work and being conscious *here and now*?', I would answer 'A vision, a quality of being, a sensation which comes in different modes and times and, in the happiest human cases, very intermittently: but which is entirely self-explanatory (though there are no words sufficient for it and I doubt there ever shall be) and vindicative of the fact of one's own existence. The appreciative among us associate this with items which, thus reeled off in a list, have to sound like—are—clichés: a sunset, an echo of water falling, the mew of a bat; forgiveness; love in its happy forms; and it is much distilled by the process of literary art, considerably crowds the imaginative pages amongst the world's written documents.

This also seems to have been Henry James's feeling: or at least that is how I read his final expostulation on the subject of his craft, the refutation of H. G. Wells's caricature of his life and work in *Boon*. (Did ever cruel manners win a richer testament for mankind's 'literary report on life'?) 'It is art that *makes* life, makes interest, makes importance, for our consideration and application of these things, and I know of no substitute whatever for the force and beauty of its process.'[12]

Emily Brontë's art takes us, we feel, several large strides

nearer to the heart of the cosmic process and in its articulation of the mortal and immortal elements at war in human nature, of Nature itself as an all-investing Power, at once so rooted in the everyday actual and so materialized in its immateriality, gives us a singular and outstanding experience in this deep kind. What would we ask for more—her blood? Art ultimately is about offering a perception of the universe where we find ourselves, which our senses are otherwise too dulled by routine and cabined by self's small confines to know, and which may convey to us part of the vision that living itself is for.

Yet I do think *an* utility-question creeps onto the scene of even our race's greatest art-works. A sterling instance is 'The Ancient Mariner'. When we have subjected ourselves fully to the (considerably disabling) revelations about spiritual life of that poem, how do we digest them? We are like its wedding-guest, sadder and wiser men the morrow morn. It also issues out of the cosmic fund and on that account alone ought to be experienced. In its power, it will inevitably change our consciousness's gear—for the duration, at least, of a reading. Rilke need not have remarked 'A great poem tells us "You must change your life".' They *do* change our lives, willy nilly. Yet just as the Mariner and his hapless victim of an auditor are put through intuitions they are only allowed to endure but cannot integrate into new, *more healthful* living, so we (witnesses also of the seaman's preternatural visitations) suffer an enlargement of consciousness which—except in the sense (a big qualification this, I agree) that it is an enlargement—does not make us more competent to cope with the here and now: an experience we do not have, I think, on rising, however battered, bloodied and bowed along every nerve, from (say) a good performance of *King Lear*.

Wuthering Heights has very much to tell us about life in the hither world. Indeed, Socialist critics lack no materials in the text for their view of it as almost entirely a political novel, a radical criticism of capitalist society. Yet at certain cruxes its leading characters yearn for a mode of being which is neither fleshly nor the (then, traditional version of the) Christian Heaven's:

> 'If I were in heaven, Nelly, I should be extremely miserable.'
> 'Because you are not fit to go there,' I answered. 'All sinners

116

would be miserable in heaven.'

'But it is not for that. I dreamt, once, that I was there.'

'I tell you I won't harken to your dreams, Miss Catherine! I'll go to bed,' I interrupted again.

She laughed, and held me down, for I made a motion to leave my chair.

'This is nothing,' cried she; 'I was only going to say that heaven did not seem to be my home; and I broke my heart with weeping to come back to earth; and the angels were so angry that they flung me out, into the middle of the heath on the top of Wuthering Heights, where I woke sobbing for joy. That will do to explain my secret, as well as the other. I've no more business to marry Edgar Linton than I have to be in heaven; and if the wicked man in there had not brought Heathcliff so low, I shouldn't have thought of it. It would degrade me to marry Heathcliff, now; so he shall never know how I love him; and that, not because he's handsome, Nelly, but because he's more myself than I am. Whatever our souls are made of, his and mine are the same, and Linton's is as different as a moonbeam from lightning, or frost from fire. . . . This is for the sake of one who comprehends in his person my feelings to Edgar and myself. I cannot express it; but surely you and everybody have a notion that there is, or should be an existence of yours beyond you. What were the use of my creation if I were entirely contained here? My great miseries in this world have been Heathcliff's miseries, and I watched and felt each from the beginning; my great thought in living is himself. If all else perished, and *he* remained, I should still continue to be; and if all else remained, and he were annihilated, the universe would turn to a mighty stranger. I should not seem a part of it. My love for Linton is like the foliage in the woods. Time will change it, I'm well aware, as winter changes the trees. My love for Heathcliff resembles the eternal rocks beneath—a source of little visible delight, but necessary. Nelly, I *am* Heathcliff—he's always, always in my mind—not as a pleasure, any more than I am always a pleasure to myself—but as my own being—so, don't talk of our separation again—it is impracticable. . . .' (Ch. 9)

David Daiches supplies a classic word of his own when he remarks, on this, that 'Emily Brontë shows no sense of the otherness of the other person in a passionate relationship between the sexes. Ultimate passion is for her rather a kind of recognition of one's self—one's true and absolute self—in the object of passion.'[13]

117

Yet the book demonstrates that sense (of the differentness of a different person) in other cases than the Catherine–Heathcliff relationship and it is, like life, equivocal as to spiritual realities. In a sense, after all, Catherine's dream and wish have come true when Lockwood first visits his landlord. The angels *have* cast her out of heaven, she is thrown back into the middle of the heath on the top of Wuthering Heights. But she is not 'sobbing for joy', the little ghost that the luckless refugee encounters in Chapter 3:

> The intense horror of nightmare came over me; I tried to draw back my arm, but the hand clung to it, and a most melancholy voice sobbed,
> 'Let me in—let me in!'
> 'Who are you?' I asked, struggling, meanwhile, to disengage myself.
> 'Catherine Linton,' it replied shiveringly (why did I think of *Linton*? I had read *Earnshaw* twenty times for Linton), 'I'm come home, I'd lost my way on the moor!'
> As it spoke, I discerned, obscurely, a child's face looking through the window—terror made me cruel; and, finding it useless to attempt shaking the creature off, I pulled its wrist on to the broken pane, and rubbed it to and fro till the blood ran down and soaked the bedclothes: still it wailed, 'Let me in!' and maintained its tenacious gripe, almost maddening me with fear.
> 'How can I!' I said at length. 'Let *me* go, if you want me to let you in!'
> The fingers relaxed, I snatched mine through the hole, hurriedly piled the books up in a pyramid against it, and stopped my ears to exclude the lamentable prayer. . . .
> 'It's twenty years,' mourned the voice, 'twenty years, I've been a waif for twenty years.'

Has Catherine in short, while on this side of the veil, got all her understanding of things inside out? Which is the better fate: to endure this animal frame as repository of a not entirely happily caged spirit-life: this-worldly, incarnated existence? *Or* the mode of being Emily Brontë intuits (and powerfully insinuates) as available beyond? If our deepest desire here is to get out of our 'bower of bone' and its limitations, shall our greatest wish (once that is accomplished) be to get back in?! On that score the novel is ambiguous with Life's own ambiguity.

Yet this is an issue which leaves all others behind, rich as the book is *in* other considerations; and it seems fair to ask what on earth the reader can do with its presentment. Make it his own, yes; drink deep at the Pierian spring: but in face of such phenomena, however accurate an account of 'life outside the body', of men's essential nature, how may one adjust his living by even a jot or tittle so as to react creatively to this intuition?

I have argued that *The Tenant of Wildfell Hall* performs a merciless daylight bombing raid on the human hope, intrinsic to most of us, that we can get our living 'right', in the sense of making happy choices with sufficient evidence, along our path through the world. It shows, and not only in Helen Hunting-don's case, that the evidence is inevitably too often *not* sufficient, can rarely be sufficient, for such an accomplishment. In that regard it is as drastic an exposé of reality at its core, the terms and conditions of human existence, as Emily Brontë's. But it does also provide a positive statement, a goal for the unleashed energies (of hope, ambition, desire for felicity) which its method has unchannelled. It informs us that all living, all human choices—however unhappy or luckless they turn out—can be rendered equally valid by being made the material of obedience and accession to the Fount itself of fulfilments.

> 'And must we never meet again?' I murmured, in the anguish of my soul.
>
> 'We shall meet in heaven. Let us think of that,' said she in a tone of desperate calmness; but her eyes glittered wildly, and her face was deadly pale.
>
> 'But not as we are now,' I could not help replying. 'It gives me little consolation to think I shall next behold you as a dis-embodied spirit, or an altered being, with a frame perfect and glorious, but not like this!—and a heart, perhaps, entirely estranged from me.'
>
> 'No, Gilbert, there is perfect love in heaven!'
>
> 'So perfect, I suppose, that it soars above distinctions, and you will have no closer sympathy with me than with any one of the ten thousand thousand angels and the innumerable multitude of happy spirits round us.'
>
> 'Whatever I am, you will be the same, and, therefore, cannot possibly regret it; and whatever that change may be we know it must be for the better.'
>
> 'But if I am to be so changed that I shall cease to adore you

with my whole heart and soul, and love you beyond every other creature, I shall not be myself; and though, if ever I win heaven at all, I must, I know, be infinitely better and happier than I am now, my earthly nature cannot rejoice in the anticipation of such beatitude, from which itself and its chief joy must be excluded.'

'Is your love all earthly, then?'

'No, but I am supposing we shall have no more intimate communion with each other than with the rest.'

'If so, it will be because we love them more, and not each other less. Increase of love brings increase of happiness, when it is mutual, and pure as that will be.'

'But can you, Helen, contemplate with delight this prospect of losing me in a sea of glory?'

'I own I cannot; but we know not that it will be so;—and I do know that to regret the exchange of earthly pleasures for the joys of heaven, is as if the grovelling caterpillar should lament that it must one day quit the nibbled leaf to soar aloft and flutter through the air, roving at will from flower to flower, sipping sweet honey from their cups, or basking in their sunny petals. If these little creatures knew how great a change awaited them, no doubt they would regret it; but would not all such sorrow be misplaced? And if that illustration will not move you, here is another:—We are children now; we feel as children, and we understand as children; and when we are told that men and women do not play with toys, and that our companions will one day weary of the trivial sports and occupations that interest them and us so deeply now, we cannot help being saddened at the thoughts of such an alteration, because we cannot conceive that as we grow up our own minds will become so enlarged and elevated that we ourselves shall then regard as trifling those objects and pursuits we now so fondly cherish, and that, though our companions will no longer join us in those childish pastimes, they will drink with us at other fountains of delight, and mingle their souls with ours in higher aims and nobler occupations beyond our present comprehension, but not less deeply relished or less truly good for that, while yet both we and they remain essentially the same individuals as before. But, Gilbert, can you really derive no consolation from the thought that we may meet together where there is no more pain and sorrow, no more striving against sin, and struggling of the spirit against the flesh; where both will behold the same glorious truths, and drink exalted and supreme felicity from the same fountain of light and goodness—that Being whom both will worship with the same intensity of holy ardour—and where pure and happy creatures both will love with the same divine affection?' (Ch. 45)

Thus, *inter alia*, Anne Brontë's riposte to the declarations of Catherine Linton (née Earnshaw)—the one who comes back as a child which has lost its way knocking at the window—in her sister's previous publication, on the subject of mortal identities and loves.

Her book does not hold to this faith simple-mindedly however. There is a season when the heroine, utterly trapped in her predicament of a life at Grassdale Manor, perceives that her very nature as a pilgrim must be assailed by its surrounding circumstances.

> I am so determined to love him, so intensely anxious to excuse his errors, that I am continually dwelling upon them, and labouring to extenuate the loosest of his principles and the worst of his practices, till I am familiarised with vice, and almost a partaker in his sins. Things that formerly shocked and disgusted me, now seem only natural. I know them to be wrong, because reason and God's word declare them to be so; but I am gradually losing that instinctive horror and repulsion which were given me by nature, or instilled into me by the precepts and example of my aunt. Perhaps then I was too severe in my judgments, for I abhorred the sinner as well as the sin; now I flatter myself I am more charitable and considerate; but am I not becoming more indifferent and insensate too? Fool that I was, to dream that I had strength and purity enough to save him myself and him! Such vain presumption would be rightly served, if I should perish with him in the gulf from which I sought to save him! Yet, God preserve me from it, and him too! Yes, poor Arthur, I will stay still hope and pray for you; and though I write as if you were some abandoned wretch, past hope and past reprieve, it is only my anxious fears, my strong desires that make me do so; one who loved you less would be less bitter, less dissatisfied. (Ch. 30)

Unsmug, not finding it easy, she clings on to Revelation—maintains her essential commitment to the promises, the strengthenings pledged in Christendom's Holy Scriptures (which have their analogues, for the matter of that, in much else of the world's religious disclosures and experience), and her life, terrible as it is, has its reliefs and remissions.

One of these is the role of Nature as comforter in the very midst of her woes. To say, with some critics, that Anne Brontë, in contradistinction to her sisters, was anti-Romantic—or even just less Romantic than they—is most unhelpful. The natural environment, whether nibbled foliage or 'the eternal rocks beneath', is not, as in Emily's pages, home and indeed fabric itself of Man's spiritual identity; but it carries through all Anne's work a central resource of

> Restoration knocking at the door
> Of unacknowledged weariness.

I quote Wordsworth there because his response to Nature has evidently fed Anne's deeply, and though (again) they differ as to pantheistic apprehensions, in all other respects the nourishment they derive from the physical world is alike. Indeed, they are united in feeling even the need to share their experiences with a loved one for those sensations to reach their fullest attainment: as the senior bard did, in the 'Lines composed above Tintern Abbey', with the company of his sister Dorothy.

> Saturday, 13th.—The week is over, and he is not come. All the sweet summer is passing away without one breath of pleasure to me or benefit to him. And I had all along been looking forward to this season with the fond, delusive hope that we should enjoy it so sweetly together; and that, with God's help and my exertions, it would be the means of elevating his mind, and refining his taste to a due appreciation of the salutary and pure delights of nature, and peace, and holy love. But now—at evening, when I see the round, red sun sink quietly down behind those woody hills, leaving them sleeping in a warm, red, golden haze, I only think another lovely day is lost to him and me; and at morning, when roused by the flutter and chirp of the sparrows, and the gleeful twitter of the swallows—all intent upon feeding their young, and full of life and joy in their own little frames—I open the window to inhale the balmy, soul-reviving air, and look out upon the lovely landscape, laughing in dew and sunshine—I too often shame that glorious scene with tears of thankless misery, because he cannot feel its freshening influence; and when I wander in the ancient woods, and meet the little wild flowers smiling in my path, or sit in the shadow of our noble ash-trees by the water-side, with their branches gently swaying in the light summer breeze that

murmurs through their feathery foliage—my ears full of that
low music mingled with the dreamy hum of insects, my eyes
abstractedly gazing on the glassy surface of the little lake before
me, with the trees that crowd about its bank, some gracefully
bending to kiss its waters, some rearing their stately heads high
above, but stretching their wide arms over its margin, all
faithfully mirrored far, far down in its glassy depth—though
sometimes the images are partially broken by the sport of
aquatic insects, and sometimes, for a moment, the whole is
shivered into trembling fragments by a transient breeze that
sweeps the surface too roughly—still I have no pleasure; for the
greater the happiness that nature sets before me, the more I
lament that he is not here to taste it: the greater the bliss we
might enjoy together, the more I feel our present wretchedness
apart (yes, ours; he must be wretched, though he may not know
it); and the more my senses are pleased, the more my heart is
oppressed; for he keeps it with him confined amid the dust and
smoke of London—perhaps shut up within the walls of his own
abominable club. (Ch. 25)

The scene's 'freshening influence', 'the means of elevating his
mind' which it offers, 'that low music' it makes, the contrast
'with him confined amid the dust and smoke of London . . .':
these are all Wordsworthian thoughts but indigenously felt
and known.

Likewise the assimilation of the landscape to human emotions or, rather, their mutual interanimation. In Chapter 45
when Markham leaves the woman he thinks he has lost,
parting as it seems indefinitely, he gives entry to 'melancholy
musings in the lonely valley' where he spends the after-time
avoiding going home, 'with the eternal music in my ears, of the
west wind rushing through the overshadowing trees, and the
brook babbling and gurgling along its stony bed'. That 'my
eyes, for the most part, [were] vacantly fixed on the deep,
chequered shades restlessly playing over the bright sunny
grass at my feet, where now and then a withered leaf or two
would come dancing to share the revelry; but my heart was
away up the hill in that dark room where she was weeping
desolate and alone' only appropriately qualifies, it does not
devalue the authorial hint of the harmonizing, the 'visionary
dreariness' Nature can afford: not as mere palliative for
human griefs alone, but as Sympathizing Messenger with

news from the heart of reality to transfigure them. We might here be wrought upon by the author of the poem 'Michael', but that the language is in this text also *sui generis*, an individually invigorating apprehension.

Ultimately we do not know whether Helen Huntingdon is right or wrong to marry Gilbert Markham (or to have married him)—as she could not know, until she has done it. But athwart that paralysis, a resource, a way of making things meaningful, is offered. Life's randomness, Reality's unbridleable Anarchism this side of the stygian moat, we can choose to make the material of submission (to God), the probation of loyalty to morality's height, the method whereby alloyed metal—the character we start our course off with—is to be refined, as Helen is refined, in the world's furnace.

That is Anne Brontë's tip. She does not put out the candle *and then leave us darkling*; and on *that* score (which is not the only one, I gladly concede) I am not sure we can say as much of her sister Emily's novel.

NOTES

1. *Screwtape Letters* (cit. supra), p. 47.
2. *Aspects of the Novel* (Harmondsworth, 1962), Ch. 5, p. 103.
3. Eagleton, op. cit., pp. 129–30.
4. See Chitham, op. cit., p. 204.
5. Cf. F. R. Leavis, *The Great Tradition* (London, 1960 edn.), p. 172: '. . . for such an upbringing as that of the young Jameses, there was a price. Never allowed to become rooted in any *milieu*, one would be remarkable indeed to develop a strong sense of society as a system of functions and responsibilities. H. J.'s interest in "civilization" betrays, tested by his actual selectiveness in the concrete field before him, a grave deficiency. "He didn't know the right people," "Q" once said to me, discussing James's criticism of the country-house. A fair point: after all, the admirable types, the public spirit and the fine and serious culture we come on when we study, *e.g.*, the *milieu* of Henry Sidgwick (intense and intelligent admirer of George Eliot) were characteristic products of the England of the "best families" in James's time. Why does he seem to know nothing about this real and most impressive best?'
   There is a lot here with which it is hard to disagree; and indeed I don't very much want to, all the more in that it seems to me our society cannot get back fast enough to emulating what was fine, *conscientious* and

creative in the Victorian mind and age. But I am not myself an '*intense* . . . admirer' of George Eliot, great novelist though she is. James (perhaps not *altogether* wittingly) finally blows the whistle on her and her associates—the complacency of their free-thinking, their self-importance and the bossy knowingness of their secularism, which all helped very much, I believe, to create the twentieth-century abyss; the Big Wars, the death-camps; with its collapse of real religious feeling and therefore morality—in practically the last thing he started, his recollections of her and G. H. Lewes, section V of *The Middle Years* (1917) and its portrait of the high demandingnesses—as to converse and consideration—of those 'gods' at their 'Witley abyss' of a villa, from anyone permitted to visit them. Oh the taking-themselves-so-seriously-schoolma'aminess of a certain seam in the Victorian intelligentsia! So that one may react with mixed feelings to Leavis's comment. In any case doesn't the greatest kind of imaginative writer, consciously or otherwise, reflect for us all society and essential considerations, out of whatever human contacts he manages to make?

6. 'Dover Beach', concluding lines.
7. See p. 37 above, in this study.
8. From G. M. Hopkins, 'The Wreck of the Deutschland', stanza 28.
9. See article on Professor Crick's latest assessment of the Darwinian evolutionary time-scale, in *The Observer* newspaper (London) for 28 February 1982.
10. Chitham, op. cit., p. 1.
11. Walter Allen, *The English Novel* (Harmondsworth, 1958), pp. 194–98.
12. Leon Edel & Gordon N. Ray (eds.), *Henry James and H. G. Wells* [*A Record of their Friendship, their Debate on the Art of Fiction and their Quarrel*] (London, 1958), p. 267, from item 70 in the volume, James's final letter, of 10 July 1915.
13. From his Introduction to the Penguin English Library edition of *Wuthering Heights* (Harmondsworth, 1965), p. 28.

4

The Letters and the Theology

What care I if good God be
If he be not good to me,
If he will not hear my cry
Nor heed my melancholy midnight sigh?
What care I if he created Lamb,
And golden Lion, and mud-delighting Clam,
And Tiger stepping out on padded toe,
And the fecund earth the Blindworms know?
He made the Sun, the Moon and every Star,
He made the infant Owl and the Baboon,
He made the ruby-orbed Pelican,
He made all silent inhumanity,
Nescient and quiescent to his will,
Unquickened by the questing conscious flame
That is my glory and my bitter bane.
What care I if Skies are blue,
If God created Gnat and Gnu,
What care I if good God be
If he be not good to me?

(Stevie Smith, 'Egocentric')

This chapter will be controversial, partisan and inflammatory of ill temper for any who have patience to read it through; but it can't be helped, 'I can do no other'—though it is not fun having fall to my lot the nastiest intellectual task, the most odious literary assignment which can be the portion of mere scribbling philosopher: justification of the Christian doctrine of Damnation.

Giving Anne Brontë's work really devoted attention, however, means taking its thought seriously; and that signifies nay-saying where there is a parting of the ways, no less than affirmation for what strikes one as true and valid in her pages. The heresy of Universalism to which she committed herself, explicitly and open-eyed, after deep thought and much inward struggle, does her feelings far more credit than writing the following paragraphs does mine. But it *is* a heresy, and its untruth can I think be argued upon this propagator's own evidence.

On the Christian view 'Many are called but few are chosen' because God is not willing to denature us of our humanity by taking away from us freedom of choice. This is a universe in which issues come to the point—cannot be indefinitely fudged and dodged and waived away in the manner of (say) the British Foreign Office. Man has the sensation of being a 'fallen' creature: the good we would do we do not and the evil we would not, that we do; this is our experience hour after hour, regularly depressing for ourselves and heavily oppressive as it is of others' lives. We can acquiesce in the curse intoning

> Oh wearisome Condition of Humanity!
> Borne under one Law, to another, bound:
> Vainely begot, and yet forbidden vanity,
> Created sicke, commanded to be sound:[1]

blame it all on the Creator and 'ignore' the problem thenceforward—but that does not make it, our badnesses go away, ameliorate our fellows' existences or give us any sense of being cleansed from elections we have made and do make, for which (in spite of being born into the condition) *we do feel personally responsible.*

This sense of responsibility is the function of our *having* a self (not simply being vegetables of an obedient unconsciant character), of possessing self-consciousness and real freedom of thought and everything else that we mean by the word identity. Sometime or other therefore during our lives, and the sooner the easier, the later the morally more fraught or complicated (in particular senses), we have to tackle head-on our besetting vices, our habitual sins, and abjure them; and according to the degree of our enslavements it will not at first

127

be easy to leave the warm swampy stewponds thereof for the chill nakedness of clear life outside their margins. But only that determined clambering out, initiated in our own wills, can bring spiritual health into our lives.

The Christian does not believe this effort will go unaided, but rather that Mighty Power rushes in spiritually to help wherever goodwill, let alone prayer, is operational. But the essential act of will lies with the individual—that is what it is or means, to have individuality—and if God were to use any other method than this one allotted to the dispensation under which we live, the unique person would cease to be as such which at present we are able to call 'I' or 'you'. It would not be our heart's own flexure which began the process of making a saint of us and fitting us for celestial harmony. We would be just pathetic plasticine zombies, squelched and remoulded by the Divine fingers. The Kingdom of Heaven that is with us here no less than hereafter has—on the Christian under-standing—one rule of entry. The members must walk in of their own free will. After that, everything else that man delights in will be added unto us. But in the first instance there is to be no coshing of passers-by in the street, lobotomizing them and dragging them indoors by main force. And what other fate is Arthur Huntingdon asking for unless he chooses his own reform, of himself?

Making the choice of self-improvement will always be painful in a degree and for a reason C. S. Lewis has well expressed:

> . . . when we have said that God commands things only because they are good, we must add that one of the things intrinsically good is that rational creatures should freely surrender them-selves to their Creator in obedience. The content of our obedience—the thing we are commanded to do—will always be something intrinsically good, something we ought to do even if (by an impossible supposition) God had not commanded it. But in addition to the content, the mere obeying is also intrinsically good, for, in obeying, a rational creature consciously enacts its creaturely *role*, reverses the act by which we fell, treads Adam's dance backward, and returns.
>
> We therefore agree with Aristotle that what is intrinsically right may well be agreeable, and that the better a man is the

more he will like it; but we agree with Kant so far as to say there is one right act—that of self surrender—which cannot be willed to the height by fallen creatures unless it is unpleasant. And we must add that this one right act includes all other righteousness, and that the supreme cancelling of Adam's fall, the movement "full speed astern" by which we retrace our long journey from Paradise, the untying of the old, hard knot, must be when the creature, with no desire to aid it, stripped naked to the bare willing of obedience, embraces what is contrary to its nature, and does that for which only one motive is possible. . . .[2]

It may be retorted 'Yes, but to punish failure in this sort with everlasting chronic torment is too severe. Is a man to outlast all the nebulae in misery inconceivable because he would not give up adultery, cards or the bottle—all of those things themselves anodynes for a central and other unhappiness, anyway, in his earthly portion—for a mere seventy years?' But what is God to do, if free will is also to be maintained? Annihilate His creature? Some of the Dominical utterances suggest that happens. Again Lewis speaks in and for his century better than some other commentators:

Our Lord speaks of Hell under three symbols: first, that of punishment ('everlasting punishment,' Matt. xxv, 46); second, that of destruction ('fear Him who is able to destroy both body and soul in Hell,' Matt. x, 28); and thirdly, that of privation, exclusion, or banishment into 'the darkness outside', as in the parables of the man without a wedding garment or of the wise and foolish virgins. The prevalent image of fire is significant because it combines the ideas of torment and destruction. Now it is quite certain that all these expressions are intended to suggest something unspeakably horrible, and any interpretation which does not face that fact is, I am afraid, out of court from the beginning. But it is not necessary to concentrate on the images of torture to the exclusion of those suggesting destruction and privation. What can that be whereof all three images are equally proper symbols? Destruction, we should naturally assume, means the unmaking, or cessation, of the destroyed. And people often talk as if the 'annihilation' of a soul were intrinsically possible. In all our experience, however, the destruction of one thing means the emergence of something else. Burn a log, and you have gases, heat and ash. To *have been* a log means now being those three things. If soul can be destroyed, must there not be a state of *having been* a human soul? And is not that, perhaps, the state which is equally well described as torment, destruction, and privation? You will remember that in the parable, the saved go to a place prepared for *them*, while the damned go to a place never made for men at all [Matt. xxv, 34, 41]. To enter heaven is to become more human than you ever succeeded in being in earth; to enter hell, is to be banished from humanity. What is cast (or casts itself) into hell is not a man: it is 'remains'.[3]

This harmonizes, rather awesomely, with Homer's description of the state of the dead in his Underworld—gibbering witless ghosts (who, significantly, need a drink of sacrificial blood to restore them to rationality). Ancient Jewry also deemed death to await no resurrection and their *Sheol*—the pit—was still more shadowy and unpleasant. For beings (ourselves) made *in potentiâ* demigods who were to be given the Morning Star and to know all species of felicity and creativity in their fullness, what definition of 'Hell' could you have worse? It is as if a Shakespeare, a Michelangelo or a Purcell should so continually have injected themselves with cocaine—for the brief spurious 'lift' it gave them—that they became irrecoverable morons just as they were about to pen or sculpt their finest works. And if the Divine Healer cancelled the effect of such riotous self-abuse with infinite persistence, He would have taken away from them the intrinsic strengths of mind and integrity of independent moral nature which made them Shakespeare, Michelangelo and Purcell in the first place.

It is not that we are not given second chances after full warnings. Earth is exactly the place where that happens. Arthur Huntingdon gains a wife who does everything humanly possible to get her husband away from alcoholic and other dissipations. Yet each time that he recovers sufficiently from the loss of bodily health which his excesses have entailed he starts again. What is Heaven to do: engage with him in an eternal Whitehall farce where he is brought back from the brink a trillion times in order to plunge over the edge ever yet again? The dawning awareness that he lived safely under such a dispensation would surely *harden* his nature in its self-indulgence, cruelty to his spouse and child, blasphemy and sloth: not work an eventual reformation. Faced as he is, instead, with the reality of not being immortal, he may have made some true act of contrition at the end (before or as or after he says 'Pray for me, Helen!' [Chapter 49, letter of 5 December]) wherewith his soul was saved alive, for all that any human onlooker can know. Nor do we perceive all the extenuating circumstances of his life—though we are informed he had a very unhappy inadequate childhood—that may plead, and effectually, in mitigation for him at the highest of courts. The whole thing is (thank Heaven) veiled from such rotten judgements as ours!

The dependence his wife expresses 'on the possibility that penitence and pardon might have reached him at the last' I beg humbly to salute; but her other reliance, the Universalist one, while it does her gentle heart credit—still more appealing are Anne Brontë's expressions of the theme in her poems and the letter of 30 December 1848 to the Revd. David Thom, D.D.[4]—yet it rings so false. Permit me again to quote Lewis, this time *his* letters—to 'Malcolm':

> If I never fled from His presence, then I should suspect those moments when I seemed to delight in it of being wish-fulfilment dreams. That, by the way, explains the feebleness of all those watered versions of Christianity which leave out all the darker elements and try to establish a religion of pure consolation. No real belief in the watered versions can last. Bemused and besotted as we are, we still dimly know at heart that nothing which is at all times and in every way agreeable to us can have objective reality. It is of the very nature of the real that it should have sharp corners and rough edges, that it should be resistant, should be itself. Dream-furniture is the only kind on which you never stub your toes or bang your knee. You and I have both known happy marriages. But how different our wives were from the imaginary mistresses of our adolescent dreams! So much less exquisitely adapted to all our wishes; and for that very reason (among others) so incomparably better.
>
> Servile fear is, to be sure, the lowest form of religion. But a god such that there could never be occasion for even servile fear, a *safe* god, a tame god, soon proclaims himself to any sound mind as a fantasy. I have met no people who fully disbelieved in Hell and also had a living and life-giving belief in Heaven.
>
> There is, I know, a belief in both, which is of no religious

131

significance. It makes these spiritual things, or some travesty of them, objects of purely carnal, prudential, self-centred fear and hope. The deeper levels, those things which only immortal spirit can desire or dread, are not concerned at all. Such belief is fortunately very brittle. The old divines exhausted their eloquence especially in arousing such fear: but, as they themselves rather naïvely complain, the effect did not last for more than a few hours after the sermon.

    The soul that has once been waked, or stung, or uplifted by the desire of God, will inevitably (I think) awake to the fear of losing Him.[5]

If the reader wishes to curse me for a smug ape complacently setting down all this theology of condemnation, let him save his breath. I write with thrills of fright rippling up and down my being at the thought of ending up (and as Helen Huntingdon points out 'soon enough') a mere psychic sediment with the end and fulfilment for which I was created lost to me. Nor do I have any confidence at all, when I review my life and behaviour hitherto, that if my soul were required of me now it would find itself standing among the sheep and not the goats. But presumably that is four-fifths of the value and point of the Dominical warnings—to betake us to our knees in terror and our lives to amendment. One cannot believe that in his dreadful prevision of the Last Day, the world's Redeemer and Judge was either uttering mere paedogogic fable ('Oh, it's all right really: I was just kidding to scare you all into virtue') or being gratuitously sadistic.

    Anne Brontë believed in Hell but as purgation, not perpetual banishment and punishment. Her belief in Heaven (to adapt C. S. Lewis's words) was obviously 'life-giving' enough to work marvels in her own life, of which we have the testimony of her letters.

    Only five of these survive that have been traced hitherto but each is a marvel of tact—self-effacement which is not (in fact really) self-regarding.

    The bulletin she sends to Smith and Elder's Reader, W. S. Williams (now deservedly famous for his part in the Brontë story) is essentially a business letter. Branwell has just died;

Williams is part of Charlotte's, not her own, publishing outlet and Charlotte is temporarily too stricken to pen an answer of her own to his latest missives.

Haworth, Sept. 29th 1848

Dear Sir,
    My sister wishes me to thank you for your two letters, the receipt of which gave her much pleasure, though coming in a season of severe domestic affliction, which has so wrought upon her too delicate constitution as to induce a rather serious indisposition, that renders her unfit for the slightest exertion. Even the light task of writing to a friend is at present too much for her, though, I am happy to inform you, she is now recovering; and I trust, ere long, she will be able to assure you herself of her complete restoration, and to give you her own sentiments upon the contents of your letters. Meantime, she desires her kindest regards to you, and participates with me in sincere pleasure at the happy effects of Mrs. Williams' seaside residence.
I am, dear Sir, Yours sincerely,
A. Brontë.

To W. S. Williams.

Look how the language is formal enough for Williams not to feel obliged to lay out expenditures of sympathy upon the Haworth family's griefs and worries, yet explanatory of the situation (Charlotte's not replying herself) and indicative of real friendliness. What would be simply too official a note otherwise, is 'redeemed' by the words 'writing to a friend' used of her sister's commercial associate. Yet there is nothing ingratiating about it. Charlotte and Anne that summer have visited him, all unexpectedly, in his London office, and in the whirl of entertainment laid on for the author of *Jane Eyre* and her sister, Williams took them, the Sunday morning, to church, in the afternoon to his mother's Bayswater home for dinner and the next day to tea in his own house where he displayed his eight children and one of Leigh Hunt's daughters sang Tuscan songs. Anne's note expresses amicality in the wake of all this but does not offer to encroach on its recipient and his glittering London contacts—or, more generally, her sister's and his association.

Her enclosure of 26 January of that year to Ellen Nussey

133

typifies (in her biographer's words) 'the usual understatement that characterized any discussion of her health. In its reticence, also, regarding the sole purpose and interest of her life at that time, the writing of *The Tenant of Wildfell Hall*, it is also characteristic.'[6]

The same tact informs her letter to Charlotte's old best school-friend written the previous autumn. Many another author would have felt justified, and not unkind for offering interesting news, in crowing over the fact that they had had one novel taken in for publication (*Agnes Grey*) and were working on another likely also to meet with acceptance. Yet not only were the Brontë sisters sworn to absolute secrecy from the world with each other about their literary achievements; Anne's note is quite void of any tone of vanity, of hidden superior self-consciousness. Look how she manages to thank Ellen for the 'kind and judiciously selected presents' in such fashion, their sender (a) is reassured that all have arrived and been satisfactorily distributed and (b) is yet not embarrassed with too effusive a gratitude. Anne conveys thanks which avoid looking (even inadvertently) as if angling for more such benefits on future occasions, and yet which are gracious and sincere. She achieves this partly by the same stroke with which she particularizes all the gifts and certifies that they have been received in safe condition by their appropriate recipients— 'from papa down to Tabby,—or down to myself, perhaps I ought to say',[7] and yet goes on about them at no greater length because Ellen is Charlotte's great friend and confidant and to do so would (again) be an act of encroachment on somebody else's achieved amity.

I have already quoted a portion of her last surviving dispatch from Haworth (on 5 April 1849). Here is its opening half:

> My dear Miss Nussy [*sic*]
> I thank you greatly for your kind letter, and your ready compliance with my proposal as far as the *will* can go at least. I see however that your friends are unwilling that you should undertake the responsibility of accompanying me under present circumstances. But I do not think there would be any great responsibility in the matter. I know, and everybody knows that you would be as kind and helpful as any one could possibly be,

and I hope I should not be very troublesome. It would be as a
companion not as a nurse that I should wish for your company,
otherwise I should not venture to ask it. As for your kind and
often repeated invitation to Brookroyd, pray give my sincere
thanks to your mother and sisters, but tell them I could not
think of inflicting my presence upon them as I now am. It is
very kind of them to make so light of the trouble but trouble
there must be, more or less—and certainly no pleasure from the
society of a silent invalid stranger—I hope however that
Charlotte will by some means make it possible to accompany
me after all, for she is certainly very delicate and greatly
needs a change of air and scene to renovate her constitution—
And then your going with me before the end of May is
apparently out of the question, unless you are disappointed in
your visitors, but I should be reluctant to wait till then if the
weather would at all permit an earlier departure. You say May
is a trying month and so say others. The earlier part is often
cold enough I acknowledge, but according to my experience, we
are almost certain of some fine warm days in the latter half
when the laburnhams and lilacs are in bloom; whereas June is
often cold and July generally wet. But I have a more serious
reason than this for my impatience of delay; *etc.*

For this document a very lengthy tribute is due; it will bear,
as it deserves, much appreciative analysis. But to crudify
marvellous delicacies of expression (i.e. of consideration) with
rough praise, let me simply remark how thoroughly this dying
woman's attention is directed to putting her *correspondent* at
ease. The letter makes no bones about its subject: her very
fraught health and this proposed scheme for its rescue or at
least her sufferings' alleviation. Yet how unharrowing, unself-
pitying it is—how she states the matter so that Ellen is not
brought into the project on any kind of false understanding.
That if she does agree, Miss Nussey must prepare herself to
find a shockingly altered, emaciated invalid, is sufficiently
insinuated in the second half of the document—quoted above
on p. 50. Yet should the whole thing fail and Anne die,
either *en route* or after the 'cure' has been tried, there cannot,
after this message, be any self-recriminations on any side or
feelings of aught other than happiness that the sick woman's
dearest wishes were accomplished. Anne writes in this regard
pressingly: for she knows that if the worst comes to the worst

Ellen will show this letter to her father and sister and coming through a third party it will reassure them more than all other words could do that her warmest earthly desire was to make the journey to Scarborough and that her spirit was prepared for other-worldly eventualities: 'I have no horror of death. . . . God's will be done.' Yet the religious content of the communication is not overblown. In *its* very restraint we have a considerateness which is an object lesson of humility.

The 'condition of complete simplicity/(Costing not less than everything)' in which that humility is grounded, is not derived from or reducible to an essential simple-mindedness. The woman who writes these letters is deeply involved in the world and its concerns. As she says there, 'I have many schemes in my head for future practise—humble and limited indeed—but still I should not like them to come to nothing, and myself to have lived to so little purpose.'[8] But that has been witnessed, much purpose accomplished, in her books.

Take *The Tenant* alone. Like her sisters' work, it is full of little subtle shocks, if read deductively: for one example out of a hundred—why have Halford (the notional recipient of the whole text) and Markham, its inditer/transmitter, temporarily fallen out (opening of Ch. 2)? Some sort of tiff there has been between them, evidently: and we infer (since Markham shows himself apt for quarrelling with people in the rest of the narrative) that more likely than not it will have been occasioned by some impetuosity on the latter's part. That in turn adds yet more ironic weight to the question, what has he (Markham) done for a career ever since he married, in Helen Huntingdon, a rich wife? (A question his narrative significantly does not answer.) If the story has illustrated anything, it is the need for people to have a full-time occupation. Arthur Huntingdon is ruined by idleness as much as liquor—the one seeks refuge in the other. Helen has always had her painting, then her housekeeping and her child's education. But when the 'hero' Gilbert gives up being a farmer, what does he take to do in its place? Perhaps gossip (or at least the sending by mail of other people's innermost confidences) and quarrelling—albeit with one whom he has found himself 'destined hereafter to become a closer friend than even [his sister]' (Ch. 2).

On this issue Anne is at one with *her* sisters. Both her novels

136

are powerful indictments of the vicious way of life of any moneyed aristocracy, the corrupted *modus vivendi* of people who have wealth and power without pressuring responsibilities for the safe disposition of those things. If this is a lesser-bourgeois type of protest (on the Marxian model), so much the better for the lesser bourgeoisie. Surely the most rational mode of life any sane social philosopher can propose is one in which all individuals are neither brutalized or tormented by poverty on the one hand, nor on the other rendered mischievous and unhappy by wealth, but, rather, have to work, without indignity, for their living. Various of the world's Socialisms propose such a state of society but usually (Marx, Engels, Trotsky, Bernard Shaw *et sequentes*) by a method that concentrates power in the hands of a few rulers who are to be unopposed in a system which has no effectual checks and balances, no tolerance of criticism or exposure to public remonstrance. Such reinauguration of the reigns of the worst Pharaohs—only now, with telegraph and machine-gun, radio and chemical 'psychiatry', made more omniscient, omnipresent and irresistible by the means of nineteenth- and twentieth-century technologies (so that you get the rule of such as Stalin, Mao etc. wherever these schemes are adopted)—the Victorian lesser bourgeoisie eschewed, and still more the British and certain other working classes, to the eternal credit of their good sense: following from which some breathing holes still remain upon this planet for its human spirits. Yet Anne Brontë's condemnation of the way of life of, the powers entrusted to, the aristocracy and landed gentry, the capitalists and upper middle classes, during her decades, is as bleak and total as any Radical could desire—just because it is (as Mr. Eagleton has pointed out) so free from personal malice and resentments. Of the three sisters hers was the longest experience in the world outside the Parsonage and the most protracted subjection to one of her society's most compromised roles, the governess. She gives the fullest exposé of what lies behind that and the *mores* prevailing through the moneyed ranks of the time, yet in a manner entirely free of veiled vindictiveness—and the more devastating an indictment it is for that.

Likewise she matches Charlotte's enterprise in exposing the horrible condition of womanhood there and then. The women in her pages go from one kind of objectionable bondage to another. The prison of their first home life is exchanged only for incarceration in marriage—which is what it amounts to, unless they are unusually lucky and gain a civilized husband: as does Esther Hargrave in Frederick Lawrence at the conclusion of *The Tenant*. But her happy ending is thrown in as a makeweight, to reassure the reader that the author is no factitious fatalist, viewing all human outcomes as unhappy on all occasions. The generality of cases, however, in that book and *Agnes Grey* makes a different point: that the female poor (e.g. Nancy Brown and her neighbours in the earlier novel) are hard-pressed just to get from one day to another making ends meet; and the middle-class ladies, when not condemned to genteel poverty (like the Brontë sisters themselves, or Agnes Grey or the fugitive Helen 'Graham') have to draw a lottery ticket in a marriage-market where there are few unpunishing prizes, in a spiritual, intellectual or emotional point of view. At the socia*lite* level marriage comes through as a claustrophobic trap—for both sexes. The role of women as chattels without legal rights or independence of any sort worth the name is underscored in every incident. That Society can act, in such circumstances, as a relentless persecutor with great efficiency, is illustrated, *inter tanta alia*, by the fate of Esther, before Lawrence (*ex machina*) rescues her; as late as Chapter 48 she is reported 'almost broken' for not making a mercenary match; and that Helen has to flee in the manner that she does, instances her lack, even as an heiress, of legal rights—whether over her own life or her child's upbringing; and therefore also how serious it is she should be persecuted by snooping neighbours in the place of her refuge.

Yet the even-handedness, the clear-headedly impassioned quality of Anne Brontë's recordation is exemplified by its satirical portrait of an unpleasant old maid, one of the local trouble-makers of Mrs. Huntingdon's scene of (as she had hoped) retirement:

> As for Richard Wilson's sister, she, having been wholly unable to recapture Mr. Lawrence, or obtain any partner rich and elegant enough to suit her ideas of what the husband of Jane Wilson ought to be, is yet in single blessedness. Shortly after the death of her mother she withdrew the light of her presence from

Ryecote Farm, finding it impossible any longer to endure the·
rough manners and unsophisticated habits of her honest brother
Robert and his worthy wife, or the idea of being identified with
such vulgar people in the eyes of the world, and took lodgings
in ——— the county town, where she lived, and still lives, I
suppose, in a kind of close-fisted, cold, uncomfortable gentility,
doing no good to others, and but little to herself; spending her
days in fancy-work and scandal; referring frequently to her
'brother the vicar,' and her 'sister, the vicar's lady,' but never to
her brother the farmer and her sister the farmer's wife; seeing as
much company as she can without too much expense, but loving
no one and beloved by none—a cold-hearted, supercilious,
keenly, insidiously censorious old maid. (End of Ch. 48)

This provokes pity too, perhaps, but the portrait here and
much earlier in the tale of Jane Wilson's general nastiness
serves to show womankind as not simply all-wronged and of
themselves inevitably faultless beings. Markham, when he
warns Lawrence against this artful baggage earlier, is not
being a snitch so much as counterbalancing the suggestion of
which the novel would otherwise be guilty; namely, that no
decisive knowledge can be arrived at, no definitive (correct)
advice, ever be gained about any human being or option.

Nevertheless, it is a bull's-eye dagger-thrust at the core of
the matter that Anne Brontë uses throughout the *The Tenant*
Marriage—so often the spinster's *locus classicus* of assumed
fulfilments and human fruitions—to show the miscalculations
and disappointments for which most of us are heading most of
the time.

What Helen Lawrence's experience demonstrates is that the
only reliable thing (on her view) in a world of constant change
and fraught choices is God's Love: and therefore the only
wholly valid aim, commitment and ambition which can be
secure of happy realization (most others will crash ruining) is
faithful service of Him athwart and through the vicissitudes of
life. This alone makes sense of the 'Fluctuations' that entitle
one of Anne Brontë's poems and the 'Vanitas Vanitatis' of
another—of which latter the metre- and rhyme-schemes themselves illustrate the continual restlessness of our mortal
condition.

In the process of that commitment Helen is purged of the

unpleasant will to dominate her husband which originally infused part of her feelings for him—as is proved by the fact that, the next time she is courted, she leaves her suitor to make the initiatives. Of itself the poignancy of that response is not lost upon us. Once bitten, almost lost. She is right now, has morally advanced, in that she lets Life go at its own pace (Markham must visit or write to her first for that relationship to resume and develop: Chs. 50–3). But that nearly costs her her next, best chance of marriage. He interprets her silence as coldness and her brother acts the part of no helpful ambassador. Significantly Gilbert does break the ice, does call at Staningley: and eventually they *are* wed. But is that good or bad news? The way the book turns upon itself and renders us unsure (having learned the tip, as it were, of complicated narrative strategies from *Wuthering Heights*) throws us back upon the sole trustworthy centre for affections and hopes:

> 'God help me now!' I murmured, sinking on my knees among the damp weeds and brushwood that surrounded me, and looking up at the moonlit sky, through the scant foliage above. It seemed all dim and quivering now to my darkened sight. My burning, bursting heart strove to pour forth its agony to God, but could not frame its anguish into prayer; until a gust of wind swept over me, which, while it scattered the dead leaves, like blighted hopes, around, cooled my forehead, and seemed a little to revive my sinking frame. Then, while I lifted up my soul in speechless, earnest supplication, some heavenly influence seemed to strengthen me within: I breathed more freely; my vision cleared; I saw distinctly the pure moon shining on, and the light clouds skimming the clear, dark sky; and then I saw the eternal stars twinkling down upon me; I knew their God was mine, and He was strong to save and swift to hear. 'I will never leave thee, nor forsake thee,' seemed whispered from above their myriad orbs. No, no; I felt He would not leave me comfortless: in spite of earth and hell I should have strength for all my trials, and win a glorious rest at last! (Ch. 33)

In that service the imperfect woman is tempered and refined; and her example, eschewing the wilfulness, holding fast to the fidelity, we should struggle to emulate. That resource, as hard-won experience, is what this author testifies to: and her *oeuvre* constitutes a rich legacy all-substantiative of the theme—on

which those of us she has left behind should feed and grow.
But for herself now, ah well,

> Jesu, heart's light,
> Jesu, maid's son,
> What was the feast followed the night
> Thou hadst glory of this nun?—
> Feast of the one woman without stain.
> For so conceivèd, so to conceive thee is done;
> But here was heart-throe, birth of a brain,
> Word, that heard and kept thee and uttered thee outright.[9]

NOTES

1. Fulke Greville, from 'Chorus Sacerdotum' (*Mustapha*).
2. C. S. Lewis, *The Problem of Pain* (London, 1940), pp. 88–9.
3. Ibid., pp. 112–13.
4. The text of that letter is reproduced on page 361 of Gérin, op. cit. There she concedes, of 'the doctrine of Universal Salvation' that 'perhaps the world is not ripe for it yet. I have frequently thought that since it has pleased God to leave it in darkness so long respecting this particular truth, and often to use such doubtful language as to admit of such a general misconception thereupon, he must have some good reason for it. We see how liable men are to yield to the temptation of the passing hour; how little the dread of future punishment—and still less the promise of future reward—can avail to make them forbear and wait; and if so many thousands rush into destruction with (as they suppose) the prospect of Eternal Death before their eyes—what might not the consequence be, if that prospect were changed for one of a limited season of punishment, far distant and unseen, however protracted and terrible it might be?

'I thankfully cherish this belief; I honour those who hold it; and I would that all men had the same view of man's hopes and God's unbounded goodness as he has given to us, if it might be had with safety. But does not that "if" require some consideration? Should we not remember the weak brother and the infatuated slave of Satan and beware of revealing the truths too hastily to those as yet unable to receive them? But in these suggestions I am perhaps condemning myself, for in my last novel *The Tenant of Wildfell Hall*, I have given as many hints in support of the doctrine as I could venture to introduce into a work of that description. They are, however, *mere* suggestions, and as such I trust you will receive them, believing that I am well aware how much may be said in favour of boldly disseminating God's truth and leaving that to work its way. Only let our zeal be tempered with discretion, and while we labour let us humbly look to God who is able and certain to bring his great work to perfection in his own good time and manner....'

My indictment of her view reads all the ungraciously harsher in the light of those remarks, and it is indeed the case that *The Tenant* carefully presents this hope ambiguously. Helen in her important debate with her aunt on the subject (Ch. 20) expresses a view which the novel as a whole neither affirms nor denies. It is not that I am concerned to discredit any part of Anne Brontë's life, personality or behaviour. (I'd have to be mad, and well might any onlooker in that case expostulate 'Who art thou that thou judgest Another's servant?') Doubtful of my worthiness to unlatch her shoes, personally, I am bothered only with the doctrine *per se*. But then I believe Ancient Eskimo are saved and now enjoy in fullness 'the light that lighteneth every man that cometh into the world', while lots of vain professors and useless *répétiteurs* of the word—can their accents be caught in *my* prose perhaps?—are far less certain of acceptation. 'Not everyone that saith unto me Lord, Lord, shall enter into the Kingdom of Heaven; but he that doeth the will of my Father which is in Heaven.' Now that *does* scare me: very much.

5. C. S. Lewis, *Letters to Malcolm: Chiefly on Prayer* (London [Fontana edn.], 1966), pp. 77–8.
6. Gérin, op. cit., p. 271.
7. Ibid., pp. 272–73, where the whole letter is reproduced.
8. Ibid., pp. 307–8.
9. Hopkins, 'The Wreck of the Deutschland', stanza 30.

Index

LT   071TSD
       SCOTT